PowerPoint 2019
Intermediate

POWERPOINT ESSENTIALS 2019 BOOK 2

M.L. HUMPHREY

SELECT TITLES BY M.L. HUMPHREY

POWERPOINT ESSENTIALS 2019

PowerPoint 2019 Beginner

PowerPoint 2019 Intermediate

EXCEL ESSENTIALS 2019

Excel 2019 Beginner

Excel 2019 Intermediate

Excel 2019 Formulas & Functions

WORD ESSENTIALS 2019

Word 2019 Beginner

Word 2019 Intermediate

ACCESS ESSENTIALS 2019

Access 2019 Beginner

Access 2019 Intermediate

CONTENTS

CONTENTS (CONT.)

Introduction

In *PowerPoint 2019 Beginner* we covered the basics of what you need to know to use PowerPoint 2019. That book focused on the core knowledge you need to navigate and use PowerPoint with an emphasis on using Microsoft's templates rather than trying to create a presentation from scratch.

While there was discussion of basic text formatting and how to present your slides, the emphasis was on letting PowerPoint do most of the work for you and keeping things simple.

Now in *PowerPoint 2019 Intermediate* we're going to take that base of knowledge and expand upon it by covering subjects such as how to add charts to a presentation, how to work with SmartArt and WordArt, adding equations, symbols, and shapes to a presentation, inserting videos and online photos, using slide transitions, and how to save presentations as PDFs or images.

We won't cover every single thing you can do in PowerPoint, but we'll get close.

And, as always, I will probably share a few opinions along the way since PowerPoint is the program I think is most prone to horrid abuse by those who value whirring and spinning special effects over a simple and straight-forward presentation of good content.

Alright then. With that said, let's get started with a refresh on basic terminology. (Keep in mind that if you're brand new to PowerPoint you may want to start with *PowerPoint 2019 Beginner* instead because I'm going to assume you already know what was covered there and skip past it quickly if it does come up.)

Basic Terminology Recap

Before we begin, I want to make sure that you know what I'm referring to when I say certain things.

Tab

I refer to the menu choices at the top of the screen (File, Home, Insert, Design, Transitions, Animations, Slide Show, Review, View, and Help) as tabs.

Click

If I tell you to click on something, that means to use your mouse (or trackpad) to move the arrow on the screen over to a specific location and left-click or right-click on the option.

If you left-click, this selects the item. If you right-click, this generally creates a dropdown list of options to choose from. If I don't tell you which to do, left-or right-click, then left-click.

Select or Highlight

If I tell you to select text, that means to left-click at the end of the text you want to select, hold that left-click, and move your cursor to the other end of the text you want to select.

Another option is to use the Shift key. Go to one end of the text you want to select. Hold down the shift key and use the arrow keys to move to the other end of the text you want to select. If you arrow up or down, that will select an entire row at a time.

The text you've selected will then be highlighted in gray.

If you need to select text that isn't touching you can do this by selecting your first section of text and then holding down the Ctrl key and selecting your second section of text using your mouse. (You can't arrow to the second section of text or you'll lose your already selected text.)

Selecting an object or text box can be done with a simple left-click. Holding down the Ctrl key will let you select a second object or text box. When an object or text box is selected you will see white circles around the perimeter.

Dropdown Menu

A dropdown menu provides you a list of choices to select from. If you right-click on a PowerPoint slide, you will see an example.

Dialogue Box

Dialogue boxes are pop-up boxes that cover specialized settings. For example, when you right-click on a PowerPoint content slide and choose Font, Paragraph, or Hyperlink from the dropdown menu that will open a dialogue box.

Task Pane

Task panes are visible around the perimeter of the main workspace, but are separate. To see one, right-click on a slide and choose Format Shape from the dropdown menu. This should bring up the Format Shape task pane on the right-hand side of the main workspace.

The task pane that displays thumbnails of your presentation slides is also always visible on the left-hand side of the main workspace.

Scroll Bar

PowerPoint has multiple scroll bars that allow you to navigate through a dropdown, task pane, or your main workspace when there is more content available than is currently visible. They are located on the right-hand side and/or bottom of your workspace when needed and along the right-hand side of your task panes when needed.

Arrow

If I ever tell you to arrow to the left or right or up or down, that just means use your arrow keys.

Slider

Some options in the formatting panes on the right-hand side or in the status bar at the bottom of the PowerPoint main screen use a slider to adjust the setting. This is a horizontal line with a wider bar perpendicular to it. If you left-click on that perpendicular bar and move it to the right or the left it will adjust that particular setting upward or downward accordingly.

You can see an example of a slider in the bottom right-hand corner of PowerPoint where there is a slider to adjust the Zoom level of the main workspace.

Import From Word

It is possible to import a Word outline into PowerPoint and have PowerPoint create your slides for you using that outline. This is a very useful trick if you're someone who tends to write your presentation outline in Word first or if you're someone who is doing a mostly text-based presentation.

If you're going to do this, the first step is to create your outline in Word using Styles. (If you don't know what Styles are, I cover that in *Word 2019 Intermediate* or you can just find it using Word's help function.)

Assign the Heading 1 Style to the title you want to use for each slide. Each Heading 1 will start a new slide in your presentation.

Assign Heading 2 to your first level of bullet points, Heading 3 to the level after that, and so on.

Once you've entered all of your text into your Word document and applied the appropriate Styles, save your Word document and close it.

Next, open your PowerPoint presentation and go to the Slides section of the Home tab. Click on the dropdown arrow for New Slide and choose Slides from Outline at the bottom of the dropdown menu.

Navigate to where your Word file is saved, select it, and choose Open. PowerPoint will then use your Word outline to create a series of slides in your presentation.

Let's walk through a quick example.

Here is what I had in Word where Important Point was using the Heading 1 Style, Important Subpoint was using Heading 2, and Important Sub-Subpoint was using Heading 3:

Important Point 1

Important Point 2

Important Point 3

Important Point 4
Important Subpoint 1
Important Subpoint 2
Important Subpoint 3
Important Sub-Subpoint 1
Important Sub-Subpoint 2
Important Sub-Subpoint 3

That imported into PowerPoint as four separate slides, because I had four entries using the Heading 1 Style.

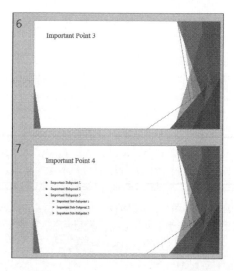

Each of the first three slides just had a title because I hadn't listed any subpoints below them.

For the fourth slide I had listed three subpoints and three sub-subpoints. Let's look more closely at that slide now:

Important Point 4

- ▶ Important Subpoint 1
- ▶ Important Subpoint 2
- ▶ Important Subpoint 3
  - ▶ Important Sub-Subpoint 1
  - ▶ Important Sub-Subpoint 2
  - ▶ Important Sub-Subpoint 3

You can see above that in addition to the title on this slide there are the six bulleted entries we would expect to see for the items where I applied the Heading 2 and Heading 3 style.

Although in this example I had all of my Heading 1 entries grouped together and then all of the Heading 2 entries after that and then the Headinng 3 after that, you do not have to do that.

I could have as easily used an outline that looked this this:

Important Point 1
Important Subpoint 1
Important Sub-Subpoint 1
Important Subpoint 2
Important Sub-Subpoint 1
Important Sub-Subpoint 2

Important Point 2

Which would have given me two presentation slides that looked like this:

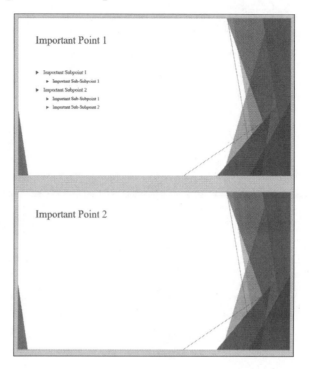

Here is a close-up of the text in the revised Slide 1:

So, basically, any Outline you can put together PowerPoint can use to make your slides for you.

Additional Text and Slide Formatting Options

In *PowerPoint 2019 Beginner* we covered the majority of the text formatting options available in PowerPoint, but there were a few that were skipped. So let's cover those now.

Text Shadowing

Text shadowing is an option that allows you to add a shadow behind your text to make it stand out on the slide. To use this option, highlight the text that you want to shadow and then click on the blurry S in the bottom row of the Font section of the Home tab.

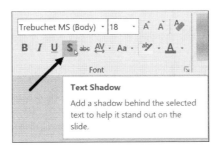

This will automatically add a shadow behind your text. You can see here an example of text that doesn't have a shadow compared to text that does:

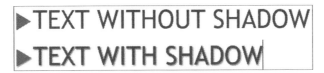

If you want to customize the shadow attributes, right-click on a word or select more than one word and then choose Format Text Effects from the dropdown menu, and then go to the Format Shape task pane and click on the arrow next to Shadow under Text Options.

The Presets dropdown menu gives you a number of pre-defined shadowed text options. It also shows how each option would look applied to the letter A.

Or you can change the settings for Color, Transparency, Size, Blur, Angle, and Distance yourself to get a customized result.

The default is for a shadow to be a black drop shadow, but depending on the settings you choose you can add a version of the text that is substantially offset from the original text or even a blurred cloud behind the text. The best way to see your options is to play around with the settings and see what happens.

Remember that Ctrl + Z, Undo, is your friend. You can always try something and if it doesn't work use Ctrl + Z to get back to where you were before.

To remove text shadowing, use the pre-set dropdown and choose the No Shadow option.

Strikethrough

You can also format your text so that it has a strike-through, which is basically a line through the text. To add a strikethrough to your text, highlight the text, go to the Font section of the Home tab, and choose the option that has an abc with a line through it.

Another option for adding strikethrough to text is to highlight the text, right-click, choose Font from the dropdown menu, and then choose Strikethrough under the Effects section of the Font dialogue box. This approach also includes a double strikethrough option which will put two lines through the selected text.

Character Spacing

An option you may need more than strikethrough is character spacing. This one is also available through the Font section of the Home tab. It's to the right of the strikethrough option and is represented by the letters AV with a two-sided arrow below them.

What the character spacing option does is adjust the amount of space between your letters.

You have five preset options to choose from: Very Tight, Tight, Normal, Loose, and Very Loose. You can also choose More Spacing which will bring up the Font dialogue box where you can specify the exact amount to expand or condense the text.

Here is an image of the difference between the default options. That top row reads "Very Tight Spacing".

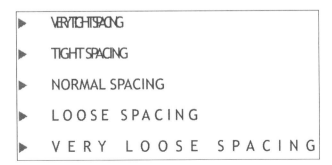

Another option for changing the character spacing is to highlight the text, right-click, choose Font from the dropdown menu, and then go to the Character Spacing tab in the Font dialogue box.

You can then choose to return the text to Normal or Expand or Condense the text using the Spacing dropdown menu. To determine the amount of spacing used, enter a value in the By box. This is the same dialogue box you'll see if you select the More Spacing option in the dropdown menu of the Font section of the Home tab.

Text Direction

In *PowerPoint 2019 Beginner* we discussed how to adjust the text direction within the context of tables, but let's just go over it again here as well, because it can be used on any text in any section of a slide.

By default, at least in the U.S., text will be oriented so that it reads from left to right in a straight line.

You can change this by highlighting your text, going to the Paragraph section of the Home tab, and clicking on the dropdown arrow next to Text Direction which will give you a choice between Horizontal (which is the default), Rotate All Text 90 degrees, Rotate All Text 270 degrees, or Stacked.

(There is also a More Options choice at the bottom of the dropdown which opens a task pane, but it doesn't allow you more choices than those four. It's more useful for specifying where on the page the text will be placed.)

Your choice of text direction will impact all text in that text box. If you need to use more than one direction on a slide, you'll need multiple text boxes.

This is what the four choices look like:

In order to actually have your text display in the direction you choose, you need to make sure that your text boxes are large enough to allow for that. For example, above with the Horizontal Text option I had a text box that was .44 inches tall. When I copied that and changed it to Rotate Text 270 Degrees, the text didn't rotate. I had to change the height of the text box to, in this case, be three inches before the text could properly display as rotated text.

You can also change the text direction by highlighting your text, right-clicking, choosing Format Text Effects from the dropdown menu, and then clicking on the Textbox option under Text Options (the far right-hand image) in the Format Shape task pane.

This will bring up the Text Box options. The second option is Text Direction which includes a dropdown with the four main choices available through the Home tab.

Here you can also choose to resize the text box to fit your text so that the issue I mentioned above isn't an issue.

Insert a Link

It's possible to link from text in your presentation to an existing file, a web page, a place in the presentation, or to launch an email to a specific email address so that when you click on that link that item automatically opens or that task is automatically performed.

For our purposes here I'm just going to discuss linking to a web page or an existing file.

To add a link to your presentation, highlight the text that you want to turn into a link and go to the Links section of the Insert tab. From there choose the Link option.

This will bring up the Insert Hyperlink dialogue box which will then give you the option to link to an existing file or web page or another place within your presentation. You can also have the hyperlink create a new document or link to an email address.

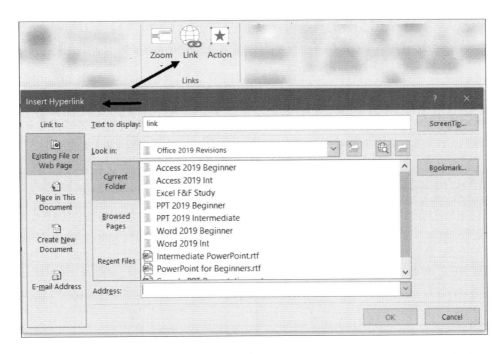

You can also open the dialogue box by selecting your text, right-clicking, and choosing Hyperlink from the dropdown menu.

The text you selected will show at the top of the dialogue box under "Text to Display". Leave this alone unless you want to amend the selected text in your presentation slide.

For linking to both files and web pages, the selection on the left, Existing File or Web Page, will already be done since that's the default.

To link to a website, add the website address at the bottom of the dialogue box where it says Address.

To link to a file use the files and folders in the middle to navigate to where the file is currently saved and click on it.

With either option you should have either a file path, file name, or a website address in the address field when you're done.

Once that's true, click on OK and PowerPoint will convert your selected text to a hyperlink.

To use the link, hold down Ctrl and click on the link. If you linked to a file it will open. If the file you wanted to link to was already opened it will take you to the beginning of the file.

If you linked to a web page, your default browser will open to that web page.

When linking files, be certain that the file will be available to open when you use the link. I have seen it happen more than once where a file was linked to a presentation but the presentation was then distributed to other users who didn't have access to the file that was linked. So, maybe it was part of a department-level shared folder that members of another department couldn't access or was on someone's laptop and so not accessible to anyone else.

This is why I generally do not recommend linking to files.

Once you have created a hyperlink, you can right-click and choose Edit Link, Copy Link, Open Link, or Remove Link from the dropdown menu. The Edit option will open a dialogue box called the Edit Hyperlink dialogue box where you can change any of the settings you want.

Copy Link will copy the link address. So, for example, for a web page you could choose to copy the link and then paste that link right into a web browser.

Open Link is another way to launch the link.

Remove Link will remove the link permanently.

Insert a Symbol

To insert a symbol, you need to click into a text box on the slide, then go to the Symbols section of the Insert tab, and click on Symbol. This will bring up the Symbol dialogue box.

(If you're not in a text box that Symbol option will be grayed-out.)

At the bottom of the dialogue box is a listing of recently used symbols. To use one of those either double-click on it or click on it and then click on Insert. The symbol will be inserted into your slide but the dialogue box will remain open until you click on the X in the top right corner to close it.

If the recently used symbols do not contain the symbol you want, you can also use the display of symbols that takes up most of the dialogue box to find the one you want. There is a scroll bar on the right-hand side. You can also choose a specific font from the Font dropdown menu. The various Wingdings fonts are usually a good source for images.

Once a symbol has been inserted into your presentation you can change any of its attributes (color, size, spacing, etc.) just like you would any other text using the Font section of the Home tab.

Use Subscript or Superscript

On occasion you may want to use a subscript (where a portion of the text is lower than the rest, think chemical notations) or a superscript (where a portion of the text is higher than the rest, think how you would write three squared, for example).

To apply a subscript or superscript to text, highlight the text you want to raise or lower, right-click, select Font from the dropdown menu, and then choose either subscript or superscript from the Effects section of the Font dialogue box.

For both options you can specify the percent to which it should be offset.

(If you're writing a lot of equations there is an easier way to do subscripts and superscripts. Look to the chapter on inserting equations for a discussion.)

Format Title Section Background

If you aren't using a PowerPoint template then the slide you're working with will just have a plain white background. In general, I wouldn't recommend this unless you're putting together a presentation that you want to print and trying to save ink because an all-white slide is very generic and boring.

One option to make a slide slightly less generic is to add a fill color to the title portion of the slide. To do this, right-click in the text box for the title section and choose Format Shape from the dropdown menu. This will open a Format Shape task pane off to the right side that allows you to add a fill to that text box. Your choices are solid fill, gradient fill, picture or texture fill, pattern fill, or slide background fill.

Click on any of those options to see additional choices related to the option. For example, if I click on Solid Fill it shows me a color dropdown option as well as a transparency slider.

Click on the arrow next to the current color to choose from one of seventy colors. You can use the More Colors or Eyedropper options to use other colors instead.

As an example, I have pasted in an image of a book cover before and then used the Eyedropper to pull the same color used in that cover to create the background color for my slides. It's a quick and easy way to make sure the colors are consistent between a book and related presentation.

Solid Fill will do just what it says and make that text box all one color.

Gradient Fill contains pre-set options for different gradients using six basic colors which you can see in the preset gradients dropdown. If one of those works for you, just click on it.

You can also choose any color you want using the Color dropdown which is available just below the gradient stops settings.

The type, direction, angle, gradient stops, position, transparency, and brightness of a gradient can also be adjusted.

The Picture or Texture Fill option comes with a set of 24 textures to choose from (most of them hideous). If you don't like any of those choices you can use your own picture by clicking on Insert under Picture Source. There you'll have a choice to find a file, online picture, or icon. Just be sure if you use an online picture that you have the right to use that picture. Just because something is on the internet does not make it free to use.

With this option you can also customize the transparency, offset, scale, alignment, and mirror type of the image.

Pattern Fill comes with 48 patterns to choose from. The colors used with those patterns are dictated by your Foreground and Background color choices. (Here is a good time to remind you to not be overwhelming with your choices and to remember some basic color principles. Also, keep in mind that some people are color blind and that using, say red and green, will mean they can't see the pattern. Not to mention it would look ugly.)

If you're expecting to put text on top of a pattern, choose a more subtle one. (Or, better yet, go with a solid color.)

Slide background fill will apply whatever the current background on your slide is to the selected text box. (So for a generic presentation, it would make it white.)

Format Slide Background

In the same way that you can add a background to a text box like the title section of a slide, you can do so to the entire background of a slide.

To do this, go to the Customize section of the Design tab and click on Format Background. This will open the Format Background task pane.

You can also right-click on the outer edge of a slide (outside of a text box) and choose Format Background from the dropdown menu which will also open the same task pane.

From there you can choose between solid fill, gradient fill, picture or texture fill, and pattern fill just like you could with a text box.

I will add the same cautions here as I did above that you need to be careful with a background fill that you don't overwhelm the presentation and make it unreadable. You have more leeway here because your text boxes will be a solid color and sit on top of whatever pattern you choose, but still. Don't distract from the words.

Here's an example where I've applied a background pattern and then used solid colors for the two main text boxes and made sure that the font color for each of those text boxes contrasted enough with the background to be visible.

Sample Presentation Text

- Important Point 1
- Important Point 2
  - Important Subpoint
    - Even more important sub-subpoint

I went with one of the more subtle background patterns but this still may be a little too busy for the average user. If you really want to be that creative, I'd encourage you to explore the provided PowerPoint templates before you try to create your own background and color scheme.

But if you want to do it yourself, that's how. The possibilities are endless. Which is a good thing when you need that and a very bad thing when you're not capable of editing yourself. Like this example:

For those of you reading in print, the color version is much much worse but even in black and white the gradients, transparency, and patterns are not helping. Remember, the presentation is there to help you convey information. If it distracts from your message so much that no one hears what you say, then you've failed.

Equations

If you're working with mathematical symbols or equations, PowerPoint actually comes with certain common equations that you can just insert into your presentation without worrying about how to find all the appropriate symbols to create them.

To use these equations, go to the Symbols section of the Insert tab, and click on the dropdown arrow under Equation.

The equations that are available pre-formatted are the area of a circle, the binomial theorem, the expansion of a sum, the Fourier series, the Pythagorean theorem, the quadratic formula, the Taylor expansion, and two trig identities, one involving the sum or subtraction of the sine of two values and one involving the sum of the cosine of two values.

To insert one of these equations into your presentation slide, click on it.

For a blank slide, the equation will insert into the slide in a text box. If you were already clicked into a text box on an existing slide, it will insert as text at the point where your cursor was.

Once you insert an equation into your presentation, an Equation Tools Design tab will also appear. It lets you build any equation you could possibly want and includes common symbols and structures that are used in equations.

Here is the Structures section of that tab:

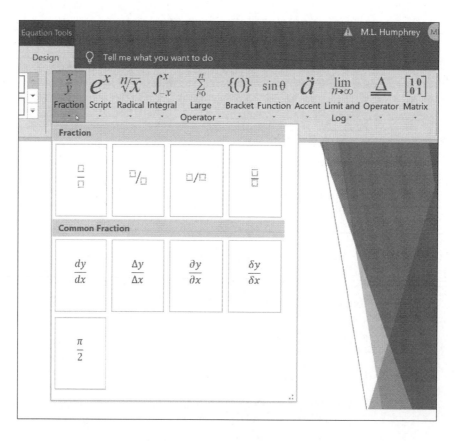

To insert a structure or symbol, simply click on it and the symbol or structure will be inserted at the point where your cursor was in the text box on that slide.

Some of the structures you insert will have dotted squares, like you can see in the Fraction section above. These allow for additional inputs. Click one of the squares and you can then add another structure or type in numbers.

Another way to bring up the Equation Tools Design tab is to go to the Equations dropdown in the Symbols section of the Insert tab and choose Insert New Equation from the bottom of the dropdown menu. That will bring up the tab and you will see text in your slide that says "Type equation here."

If you have a stylus or are just very good at writing with your mouse (I certainly am not), you can also choose the Ink Equation option. This will pop-up a dialogue box where you can "write" the equation and PowerPoint will convert it into typed text. I was able to get it to do 2+3 for me. Without a stylus I'm not sure I could write a big calculus formula, though. But it is an option.

Okay.

For each equation there are three display options available in the Tools section on the left-hand side of the Equation Tools Design tab: professional, linear, and normal. Here is an example of the area of a circle equation written in each format:

> ▶ **Professional:** $A = \pi r^2$
>
> ▶ **Linear:** $A = \pi r \wedge 2$
>
> ▶ **Normal:** $A = \pi r^2$

To edit an existing equation, click anywhere within the equation to make the Equation Tools Design tab available and then choose your preferred format.

You can also change the size of the text in your equation by selecting the text and then using the Font section of the Home tab like you would with any other text. If the text is formatted as Professional you can't change the font from Cambria Math, but you can still change the font size and add bolding, italics, etc.

WordArt

Now we come to WordArt, which for a normal corporate presentation is probably not a good idea. Remember the whole adage about not letting the presentation get in the way of what you're presenting.

But there will be people who want to use it. And there may be settings in which it makes sense to do so. (I know a few people who, for example, design book covers in PowerPoint.)

So. Let's cover it.

What WordArt does is inserts text into your presentation that has various enhancements added such as a fill color, border color, and/or shading. Or, sometimes, all three. Like here:

Your text here

You can insert WordArt by going to the Text section of the Insert tab and choosing from the WordArt dropdown menu.

Initially you'll have twenty choices of format to choose from. Click on one of those choices and PowerPoint will insert a text box with that formatting that includes the words "Your text here". You can then replace that text with your own and it will keep the formatting you chose.

Another way to get to the same formatting options is to type text into a slide and then use the Drawing Tools Format tab, which should be visible as long as you're clicked onto your text. It has a WordArt Styles section that includes those twenty pre-formatted options as well as dropdowns for Text Fill, Text Outline, and Text Effects.

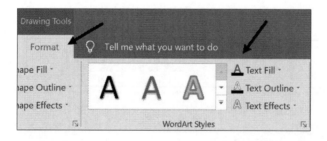

By making selections from the Text Fill, Text Outline, and Text Effects dropdowns in the WordArt Styles section of the Drawing Tools Format tab you can create a completely customized style for your text.

If you click on the expansion arrow for the WordArt Styles section that will open the Format Shape task pane. For me it defaulted to a section that had the Text Effects options. The Text Fill and Text Outline options were in a separate section to the left of the Text Effects. You can also open that pane by right-clicking on your text and choosing Format Text Effects from the dropdown menu.

So, what are your options?

Text Fill allows you to change the surface of the letters to be any solid color, a gradient, or a texture. You can also use a photo for the surface of your text.

If you want to use a gradient that is a specific color, so let's say shaded green text, you need to choose the color first and then the gradient option because otherwise choosing the color will convert it back to a solid color.

I kind of find their texture options hideous, but the picture option would allow you to bring in any texture you'd like to use on your letters. (Or you can in fact use a real picture. I've seen that done on book covers.)

The Text Outline option allows you to add or change the color, weight, and style of the line used along the border of each letter. If you use the task pane there are options for transparency (which will make the border appear lighter in color than your selected color choice) and additional line types.

The Text Effects option allows you to apply a shadow, a reflection, a glow, a bevel, a 3-D rotation, or a transformation to your text. Transformations place text along a path or "warp" the text into various shapes. You can see the options in the secondary dropdown menu.

If you use the curved text effect, you will likely need to adjust the size of the text box to get the text to curve the way you want it to. You may also need to force text onto different lines or add extra spaces if trying to create a circle of text like this one:

So a lot you can do with WordArt. It's fantastic for things like creating a logo or some other artistic imagery. But it should still be used with caution for a basic professional presentation.

Alright. Now let's talk about shapes.

Shapes

Insert Shapes

You can also insert a wide variety of shapes into your presentation. This can be done via the Drawing section of the Home tab, the Insert Shapes section of the Drawing Tools Format tab, or the Illustrations section of the Insert tab (under the Shapes dropdown). Here is what the option looks like in the Home tab:

If you click on the down-pointing arrow with a line above it, you'll see a much larger set of shapes to choose from. They fall into the categories of Recently Used Shapes, Lines, Rectangles, Basic Shapes, Block Arrows, Equation Shapes, Flowchart, Stars and Banners, Callouts, and Action Buttons.

The most common shape I insert is the first one shown, which is a text box. It's the A in the corner of a box with lines in it.

To insert a text box into your presentation slide, click on the text box option and then click onto your presentation slide. The inserted shape will be equivalent to one character. You can then type text and it will expand in size as you type.

You can also left-click and drag to the side and up or down to create a text box before you start typing. This can be especially useful when you're not yet ready to add text, but do want to define the space in which you plan to add text.

The same process works for other objects as well. So if I want to insert a downward pointing arrow, I just select that option from my menu and then either click onto my presentation slide or click and drag to get the size I want.

If you have issues inserting a text box or other shape into your presentation slide, try inserting it in an area that doesn't already have a text box in it and then dragging the text box to where you want it to go.

Some shapes may require multiple clicks to create or may require that you left-click and hold as you move your cursor around to draw them.

For example:

Scribble requires a left-click and hold as you then scribble on your slide.

Freeform: Shape will close and complete once you connect your last point to your beginning point, You can either click and hold as you create a scribbled shape that connects back to the starting point or you can click multiple times to create a series of straight lines that are only complete when you click back on the origin.

Curve will anchor and curve your line from the anchor point each time you click on the presentation. You'll see the curve when you move your mouse away from each anchor point. It will only stop making new curves when you use Esc or Enter or connect back to the origin.

Change Shape Size

To change the size of an inserted shape or object, you have a few options. If you click on it you'll see white circles around the perimeter. You can click and drag on one of those white circles to change the height or width of the object. If you want to do so proportionately, click on one of the circles in the corner and drag at an angle.

You can also use the Size section of the Drawing Tools Format tab. By default it will change height and width separate from one another so skew your shape.

A better option if keeping the shape's proportions the same matters, is to right-click and choose Format Shape from the dropdown menu.

This will open the Format Shape task pane. Click on the Size & Properties choice under Shape Options and then expand the Size dropdown. The checkbox there for Lock Aspect Ratio will ensure that when you adjust the height the width also adjusts or vice versa.

You can then adjust the height or the width value and know that the other value will adjust as well to keep the image the shape the same as you increase or decrease its size.

Adjust Shape Form

For shapes that consist of multiple curves or lines, you can also adjust the individual segments.

For some shapes, like arrows, you will have one or more yellow circles that appear when you click on the shape. You can click on that yellow circle and drag to change the location of the anchor point. For arrows this lets you make the base of the arrow wider or narrower or change where the point of the arrow begins.

For other shapes, like Scribble, you can instead right-click and choose Edit Points from the dropdown. This will place a number of black boxes along the outline of the shape. You can then click on any of those boxes and drag them to alter the shape.

Edit Points is also available in the Insert Shapes section of the Drawing Tools Format tab under Edit Shape.

For a line with an arrow at the end, you can change the direction the arrow is pointing by clicking and dragging the white circle at the pointed end.

For a two-dimensional arrow you can change the direction of the arrow along a straight line that way (so left to right, top to bottom), but to rotate it to the side you'd need to use the rotation option that appears along the edge of the shape. (An arrow that forms a circle pointing to the right. Click on it and drag.)

You can also flip horizontal or vertical or rotate 90 degrees using the Rotate option in the Arrange section of the Drawing Tools Format tab.

Choose More Rotation Options from the bottom of that dropdown to open the Format Shape task pane where you can change the rotation to any degrees between -3600 and 3600. (Although 0 to 360 is actually all you need).

Note that the degree of rotation is based upon the starting point of the shape. So if you had an arrow that was already pointed off to the right then a rotation of ninety degrees would have that arrow pointing downward since that's ninety degrees from where it started.

Change Shape

You can change an existing shape to a different one by clicking on it and then going to the Drawing Tools Format tab and choosing Edit Shape from the Insert Shapes section and then choosing Change Shape which will show you all available shapes. Select the one you want.

Fill, Outline, and Effects

Just like with WordArt, you can change the fill, outline, and effects for a shape. First, click on the shape you want to change and then go to the Drawing Tools Format tab.

There are a number of pre-formatted Shape Styles that you can choose from in the Shape Styles section.

The colors used there will be colors that match your chosen theme. Hold your mouse over each one to see it applied to your shape. Click on it to permanently apply it.

You can also find these options under the Quick Styles dropdown in the Drawing section of the Home tab.

If you want more control over the appearance of your shape, you can use the Shape Fill, Shape Outline, or Shape Effects options available in those same sections.

The Shape Fill, Shape Outline, and Shape Effect options work the exact same way as the Text Fill, Text Outline, and Text Effects options did with WordArt. Your default color choices will be related to the theme colors. You can click on More Colors to choose any colors you want.

Just, you know, remember your audience and don't get too carried away.

Move Shapes Relative to One Another

If you have more than one shape in a presentation slide then you're probably going to end up wanting to move those shapes around relative to one another.

This is done using the Arrange options which are available either in the Drawing section of the Home tab or in the Arrange section of the Drawing Tools Format tab.

The Align object options are located in the secondary dropdown menu in the Position Objects section.

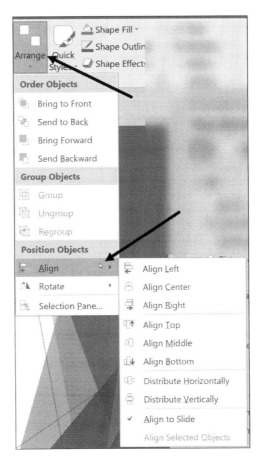

You can also just right-click on shapes to bring them forward/back or to group them once you've selected more than one.

Bring Forward/Send Backward

To change the order of overlapping objects, use bring to front, send to back, bring forward, and send backward options.

When dealing with bringing shapes forward or moving them backward, think of the shapes as stacked one on top of the other with the "top" of the stack in the front. This is the layer that will be fully visible. If that shape overlaps another shape then where the two overlap you will only see the topmost shape. Any portion of the other shape will be hidden.

You can either move a shape one level at a time (with bring forward or send backward) or all the way to the front or back at once (with bring to front or send to back).

You might use this, for example, if you had a triangle and a text box on a slide and wanted to put the text box on top of the triangle. To make this work, you might need to tell PowerPoint to move the text box forward so that it was visible on top of the triangle or to move the triangle backward so that it was behind the text box.

Group Objects

To group or ungroup objects use the Group, Ungroup, and Regroup options.

Group takes multiple shapes that you've selected and lets you move them around or resize them as one unit. So, for example, with that text box and triangle combination, I'd want to group those two elements once I had them properly aligned to one another so that if I had to resize or move them I wouldn't lose that work.

Align Objects

And then there's a whole set of options for positioning objects that lets you align those objects to one another or to various portions of the presentation slide.

The alignment options are align left, center, right, top, middle, or bottom as well as distribute horizontally, distribute vertically, and align to slide.

Whichever alignment choice you make will only include the shapes you select. The other shapes on the slide will not move.

If you choose the option at the bottom of the dropdown to Align Selected Objects, then the selected objects will align relative to one another.

If you choose to Align To Slide instead, then the slide will basically be treated as another shape and your shapes will align to it.

Which direction your shapes move to align will depend on their position relative to one another and the alignment choice you make. So align left will move all shapes to align along the left-most edge of the left-most shape. Align right will move all shapes to align along the right-most edge of the right-most shape. Align middle will move all selected shapes to align along the midline between the left-most edge and the right-most edge of those shapes.

Here is an illustration of the six alignment choices using two equally-sized but offset arrows to demonstrate. The middle, lighter-colored, row of arrows shows the original position of the arrows. The top row has the results of applying Left, Center, and Right to those arrows. The bottom row has the result of applying Top, Middle, and Bottom.

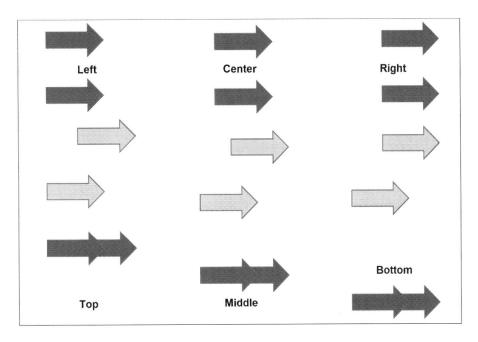

In the top row the arrows have moved horizontally. For Left you can see that both arrows moved so that they were aligned along the left-most side of their combined space. For Center they both aligned along the center point of their combined space. For Right they aligned along the rightmost edge of their combined space.

On the bottom row the arrows have moved vertically. For Top they aligned along the topmost edge off their combined space. For Middle they aligned along the midline of their combined space. And for Bottom they aligned along the bottom edge.

Distribute Horizontally will distribute the selected objects equidistant along a horizontal line within their combined space. Distribute Vertically will do so along a vertical line.

These were objects aligned to one another. If I'd instead aligned them to the slide then they would have been moved relative to the area of the slide or the active workspace of the slide.

Selection Pane

If you have a large number of shapes on a presentation slide, you can use the Selection Pane which is available in the Arrange section of the Drawing Tools Format tab. Clicking on this option will open a new task pane on the right-hand side of the screen that shows every single shape on that slide. You can then select any of the shapes that you want to group or align from that pane rather than trying to select them on the presentation slide itself, although the names PowerPoint assigns each object may not be all that helpful.

To close this pane just click on the x in the top corner.

(If you ever need to select all of the objects on a presentation slide at once, Ctrl + A also works. Just be sure to click outside of any text boxes before doing so or it will just select all of the text in the text box instead of the objects on the slide.)

Action Buttons

There is a special type of shape that you can insert into a presentation that's called an action button. They're available in the very last section of the shapes dropdown menu.

To see what each one does, hold your mouse over it. For example, the first item in that list is described as "Action Button: Go Back or Previous".

Once you insert an action button you can click on that button to perform the specified action.

Unlike the other shapes, when you insert an action button into your presentation this will open a dialogue box where you then need to provide additional information so that the action represented by the shape can be performed.

There is a dropdown menu available in the Action Settings dialogue box that allows you to choose different actions than just the default. You can set an action button to take you pretty much anywhere in your presentation or another presentation or a URL address or even open a file.

The dialogue box that you'll see for each action button is the same one but the default settings will be different depending on the action button you selected.

For example, the sound action button has by default the play sound option checked and an applause sound file selected. (Again there is a dropdown menu provided with numerous sounds to choose from including a custom sound file.)

You can either set an action to occur when you click on it or when you move your mouse over it. The default is for the action to occur when you click on the action button.

To change the settings for an action button you've already placed in your presentation, right-click on the action button image and choose the Edit Link option from the dropdown menu or click onto the action button and then choose Link from the Links section of the Insert tab.

Also, the appearance of an action button can be modified the same way any other shape can be modified so you don't have to stick to the default shape that PowerPoint uses for that action.

Rulers, Gridlines, and Guides

Okay, now let's talk about a few tools that will assist you in positioning your elements on a presentation slide visually instead of by using the alignment options. Namely, rulers, gridlines, and guidelines.

If you go to the Show section of the View tab you'll see that there are three options listed on the left-hand side: ruler, gridlines, and guides. If the boxes are checked, they're in use, if they're not checked they're not in use.

You can also right-click outside of a content box on any presentation slide to see options for Grid and Guides and for Ruler in the dropdown menu.

When gridlines are turned on you should be able to see very subtle dotted lines in the background that intersect to form equally-sized squares across the entire presentation slide except at the edges where the squares are only partial squares. Each complete square is one inch by one inch.

These lines are not visible during a presentation or when the presentation is printed, but when I'm dragging items around on a presentation slide. I will often align the items along these gridlines.

Guides are lines that run across the slide at any point you specify. They can be either horizontal or vertical. To add one, right-click on your presentation slide, go to Grid and Guides, and then choose Add Vertical Guide or Add Horizontal Guide. The guide will initially be placed in the exact center of the slide and will be a dotted line that goes off the edge of the slide.

To move a guideline, hover your mouse over it until you see two parallel lines with arrows pointing out from them, then left-click and drag. As you drag the guideline you should see a number. This number indicates how far the line is from the center point of the presentation. The directional arrow next to the number indicates the direction from the center point.

M.L. Humphrey

So a right arrow next to a 1.25 means that the guideline is 1.25 inches to the right of the center of the slide.

Guidelines are also not visible during a presentation or on a printed slide. They are just meant to help you place the elements in your presentation.

The Ruler option will add a ruler along the left-hand side and top of the presentation. The ruler is numbered from the center point of the slide. So you can see that it will go from say 6.5 to 6.5 with a mid-point of zero.

Rather than adjust the size of a shape in the Drawing Tools Format tab by specifying a value, I will often just click and drag and use the gridlines, guidelines, or ruler to determine where to stop.

Headers and Footers

You can add headers or footers to your slides or handouts fairly easily. For slides you can only add a footer, for handouts it's a header and/or a footer.

To do so, go to the Text section of the Insert tab and click on Header & Footer. This will bring up the Header and Footer dialogue box.

You can also reach the Header and Footer dialogue box by clicking on either the Date & Time or Slide Number options in the Text section of the Insert tab.

There are two tabs available in the dialogue box, one for your slide and the other for notes and handouts.

You can add three different items to the footer of a slide: date and time, slide number, and/or custom text (under the Footer heading).

For date and time, click on the box next to where it says Date and Time. Be very careful here if you choose to update automatically because that may not be what you actually intended. If you make that choice then every single time the document is opened the date and time will change. This is a mistake I often see made with memo fields where people use automatic date and time and then forget they've done so and the date on the memo keeps changing every time someone opens it.

The other option is to choose a fixed date and input the date you want.

You can include the slide number at the bottom of a slide by clicking on the checkbox next to Slide Number.

You can also insert customized text in the footer by checking the box next to Footer and then typing in whatever text you want.

The final item on the slide tab indicates whether you want those items included on your title slide. I usually do not.

You can see where each item in the footer will be placed in the preview on the right-hand side of the dialogue box. This varies by template. For the template I'm currently using, the Footer text was placed in the bottom left, the date towards the bottom right, and the slide number a little further to the right. When I switched it to a different template the date went in the left, the text went to the right, and the slide number stayed on the far right.

(You can adjust these placements by editing the Master Slides for the template, which we'll discuss later. Just be careful if you do that. It can go wrong fast.)

Finally, you can either apply your footer to that specific slide by choosing Apply or to all slides in your deck by choosing Apply To All. Usually you'll want to apply to all.

To add a header or footer to your notes and handouts, click on the Notes and Handouts tab in the dialogue box instead. You can then add the date and time, a page number, a customized header, or a customized footer to your notes and handouts.

Remember, this is not for the presentation itself, but rather for the notes or handouts that can be generated related to the presentation.

Once more, the preview off to the side will show you where each element will appear on the document. As you click on an item its location will be outlined with a darker border. But you need to pay attention to see which one it is because if you have more than one item checked there will be more than one location outlined with a darker border. You can check and uncheck the boxes to see the location for each item if you really need to.

Charts

Now let's talk about how to insert a chart into a presentation.

Insert a Chart

To insert a chart, you can bring up a content-type slide and then click on the second image on the top row which looks like a column chart with three columns. If you hold your mouse over the icon it will say Insert Chart.

You can also go to the Illustrations section of the Insert tab and choose Chart from there.

Whichever you choose, this will bring up the Insert Chart dialogue box.

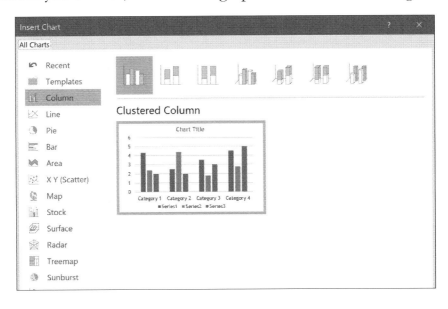

(If you're familiar with Microsoft Excel, you'll notice that this is almost identical to the dialogue box that you see in Excel when you choose to insert a chart.)

The main chart types are displayed along the left-hand side and the sub-types of those charts are along the top. Click on any chart to see a sample displayed in the main area of the dialogue box.

By default, when a chart is inserted into your presentation the colors will match your chosen theme.

To insert a chart into your presentation, click on the chart type you want, and then click on OK in the bottom right corner of the dialogue box.

So, for example, if I want an X Y scatter chart with markers, I'd click on X Y (Scatter) on the left-hand side and then click on the second or fourth option up top depending on whether I wanted my data points connected with a curved or a straight line.

Once you click on OK, PowerPoint will insert that chart type into your slide and show you a pre-populated data table in a spreadsheet window that uses dummy data. Replace that data with your own and you will have a completed chart.

For me just now the spreadsheet window was too small to show the data, so I had to move my cursor to the lower edge of the window until I could see a two-sided arrow and then I left-clicked and expanded that window until I could actually see the data.

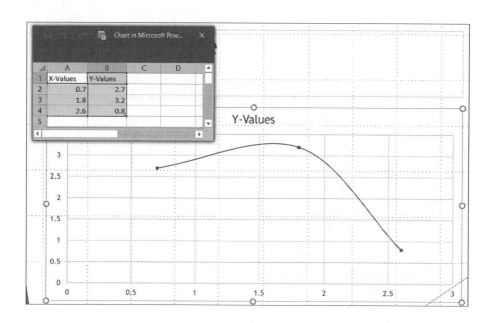

We'll return to how to change that data later, but first I want to discuss the different chart types you have to choose from.

For those of you who have already read *Excel 2019 Intermediate* or *Excel 2019 Charts* you can skip this section because it's going to be the same. For those who aren't familiar with the different types of charts, read on.

Note that I am only covering here the most common chart types: column, bar, line, pie, doughnut, and scatter.

Chart Types

Column Charts

The first chart option listed is Column. There are seven possible column charts that you can choose from, but I'm going to focus on the first three choices, which are the 2-D versions, since most of the 3-D versions are the same except three-dimensional.

For 2-D, you can choose from clustered columns, stacked columns, and 100% stacked columns. Here is an example of all three using the exact same data:

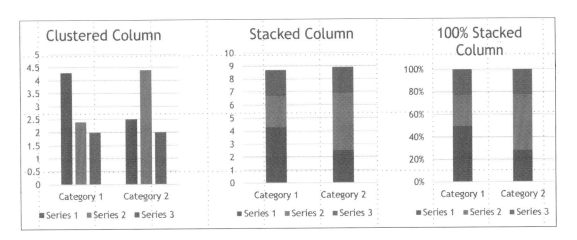

The difference between the clustered columns and the stacked columns is that the clustered columns version puts the results for each series side-by-side for each category.

You can easily see the height difference between different results, but it can quickly become too busy if you're dealing with a large number of entries.

For example, I have nine sales channels I track across months. Having nine columns side-by-side for each of twelve months would be overwhelming.

(I'm using series and category here even though those aren't the most comfortable terms for me because that's what PowerPoint uses as the defaults when it builds a chart. For me, Category is generally a time period and Series is generally one of my vendors or one of my titles. So I'll do a column chart of sales per title per month or sales per vendor per month. Just wanted to mention that in case it helps you as well since I don't think most people think in terms of series across categories. Anyway.)

For me the stacked columns option is a better choice than the clustered columns choice. Like with clustered columns, stacked columns have different column heights for each series based on their value, but the columns are stacked one atop the other for each category instead of shown side-by-side which means you end up with only one column per category.

The stacked columns option lets you see the overall change from time period to time period based on the total height of the column as well as for each variable based upon its absolute size as part of that column.

The final option, the 100% stacked columns option, presents all of the information in one column just like stacked columns does. But instead of basing each section's height on its value, it shows the percentage share of the whole.

While you lose any measurement of value (a column chart with values of 2:5:5 will look the exact same as one with values of 20:50:50 or 200:500:500), you can better see changes in percentage share for a given series. (A variable that goes from 10% share to 50% share will be clearly visible.)

As mentioned above, the first three 3-D column chart options are the same as the 2-D options. The only difference is that the bars are three-dimensional instead of two-dimensional. This can sometimes make a chart in a PowerPoint presentation more dynamic, but it can also come off as gimmicky, so use it with caution. My preference is to use charts that keep the focus on the data and not my fancy schmancy presentation skills.

The final 3-D option is a more advanced chart type that creates a three-variable graph. I'm not going to cover that in further detail here since it's more of an advanced topic, but know that it is available for those who want it.

Line Charts

Line charts are the next chart type. There are again seven options listed, but I would recommend if you're not sure what you're doing to only use the first and the fourth options, which are line and line with markers.

These are the standard line graph most of us are used to where the line height corresponds to the values of what's being charted.

The other options are line graph equivalents of the stacked and 100% stacked column graphs. In 2020 I did see a fair number of these actually used for charting outcomes by age group where there was a line for each age group and the height of the top-most line was the overall occurrence.

However, each time I saw those used I also saw that the area under each line was filled in with color so that it was not just plain lines on the chart. I'd still strongly recommend against using the stacked and 100% stacked options as plain lines. If you do use them, fill in the space below the lines to make it clear that the lines are not absolute values.

The 3-D line chart option is a more advanced chart type that creates an actual three-variable line graph and we're not going to cover that here. You can use it to create a two-variable line graph with a three-dimensional line, but don't. Keep it simple.

Here are examples of the basic line chart and the line chart with markers:

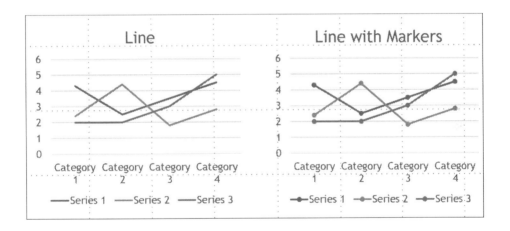

Pie and Doughnut Charts

Next we have pie and doughnut charts, which are both listed under the heading of pie charts.

Pie and doughnut charts are best used when are looking at only one series per category. So, for example, I use them for annual results by title or by vendor. The sample charts PowerPoint provides show quarterly results.

There are three two-dimensional pie chart options, one three-dimensional pie chart option, and one doughnut chart option.

The three-dimensional pie chart option is the same as the basic pie chart except in three-dimensions. The doughnut chart is basically a hollowed out version of a basic pie chart.

Here are examples of the three two-dimensional pie chart options:

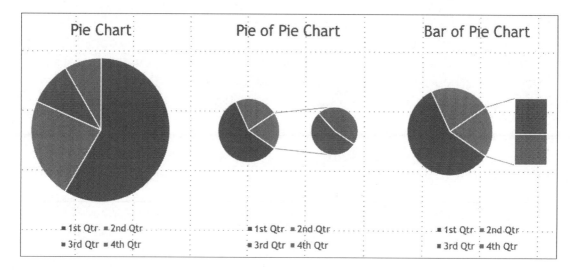

You can choose between a standard pie chart, a pie of pie chart, or a bar of pie chart

If you're only focused on who or what accounts for the biggest share, then you should just use the standard pie chart or the doughnut chart.

If you want to be able to clearly see the results for all of your segments, even the smallest ones, then the pie of pie chart or the bar of pie chart are potentially better choices.

The pie of pie chart creates one main pie chart in which it combines a number of the smaller results to form one segment of the chart. It then breaks out those smaller results into their own pie chart where they each take up their proportion of that smaller part of the pie.

So, for example, in the sample we're seeing here, 3rd quarter and 4th quarter were combined in the left-hand pie chart. 1st quarter is 58%, 2nd quarter is 23%, and then 3rd and 4th quarter combined are 19%. In the second pie chart you have 3rd and 4th quarter. 3rd quarter is only 10% of all four quarters, but 53% of the combination of the 3rd and 4th quarter values so in the second pie chart it shows as a little more than half of that pie chart.

Personally, I find it visually confusing. You can adjust the size of the secondary pie chart to help with that issue, but it's still something that I have to stop and think about.

The bar of pie chart does something similar except it creates a bar chart with the smaller values instead of a pie chart.

In order to avoid confusion, the bar of pie chart is probably the better choice of the two, but honestly I wouldn't use either one if you can avoid it. (The best charts can be read without explanation and I'm not sure that would be true for either of these for your average user. Maybe for a specialized audience where these types of charts are used often, but be wary.)

Also, if the secondary chart doesn't include the results you think it should, sort your data table from largest to smallest and see if that fixes the issue.

Bar Charts

Your next option is a bar chart. Bar charts are just like column charts, except on their side, with a clustered, stacked, and 100% stacked option available in both two-dimensional and three-dimensional versions.

Scatter Charts

The final chart type I'm going to cover here is the X Y or scatter chart (or plot).

Scatter charts plot the value of variable A given a value for variable B. There are five scatter plot options as well as two bubble plot options. We're not going to discuss the bubble plot options here.

The first scatter plot option is the classic scatter plot. It takes variable A and plots it against variable B, creating a standalone data point for each observation. It doesn't care what order your entries are in, because there's no attempt to connect those entries to form a pattern.

The other four scatter plot options include lines drawn through each plotted point. The two smooth line options try to draw the best curved line between points. The straight line options just connect point 1 to point 2 to point 3 using straight lines between each point. The charts with markers show each of the data points on the line, the charts without markers do not.

PowerPoint draws the line from the first set of coordinates you provide to the second to the third, etc. This introduces a time component into your data since the order you list the data points in impacts the appearance of the line. If you have data where the order of the measurements doesn't matter and you still want to draw a line through the points, then you'll want to sort your data by one of the variables before you create your scatter plot.

Here is an example of a basic scatter plot, one with straight lines, and one with smooth lines that uses markers:

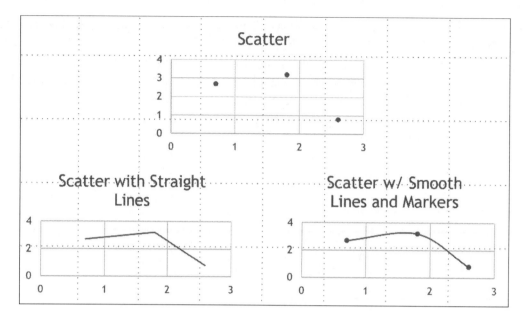

You can also use scatter plots to chart more than one set of results. You just need to add another column to the provided data table so you can input the values for the second set of results. (The spreadsheet provided by PowerPoint is going to work just like it would in Excel. The only difference is that PowerPoint gives you a data table to start with whereas Excel does not.)

Entering Data via PowerPoint

I would highly recommend that if you're going to work with charts in PowerPoint that you become familiar with working with them in Excel. Because basically that's what you're doing. The chart you create just happens to be displayed in PowerPoint.

When you insert a chart into PowerPoint it gives you a data table with pre-filled values. You can simply type over those values by clicking into the cells in the provided spreadsheet and replacing them with your values. Another option is to copy and paste your data from Excel into the data table provided by PowerPoint.

For me the data table often opened as too small a window to actually see the data. If that happens to you, just increase the size of the Excel window until you can see everything.

You can also paste in more data than is in the sample. For example, I took the pie chart that by default has four values and pasted in seven values just fine.

(The chart will update immediately. If it updates fine but you can't see your new data in the Excel window, check your formatting for those cells.)

If you already inserted the table and now need to edit the data for that table, either right-click on the chart and choose Edit Data from the dropdown menu or click on the chart and then go to the Data section of the Chart Tools Design tab and click on the dropdown for Edit Data there.

Your choices are to Edit Data or Edit Data in Excel. For me both options open a small Excel window with a name of Chart in Microsoft PowerPoint.

The data that's already being used in the chart will be shown, just overwrite or edit that. If you need to add more data than is currently being used, do so in the same columns as the existing data.

Importing An External Chart

Another option is to just do everything in Excel and then copy and paste the chart you created in Excel into your PowerPoint slide. I just did that and the chart even pasted into PowerPoint using my theme colors.

I was also able to change the colors, fonts, etc. of the pasted chart once it was in PowerPoint. But be careful because when I tried to Refresh my data it erased all my values.

When you paste from Excel instead of designing your chart in PowerPoint, the data behind the chart is still in that Excel spreadsheet, not PowerPoint. So when you choose to Edit Data, you will be editing data in your source worksheet. (Which means there's a potential to break your presentation if that file is no longer available.)

It's not the best option, really, but very quick and easy for those of us who are more comfortable in Excel than PowerPoint. I'd probably only use it for charts I know are done and ready to go and then I'd paste them in as Pictures that can't be edited at all. But at least they wouldn't break if I moved or renamed the source file. And no one would be able to refresh them and erase all their data.

Change Chart Type

To change your chart type, right-click on the chart and choose Change Chart Type from the dropdown menu.

You can also click on the chart and then click on Change Chart Type in the Type section of the Chart Tools Design tab.

Either way this will open the Change Chart Type dialogue box where you can select your new chart type and then click on OK to apply the change.

Keep in mind when changing chart types that certain chart types, like column and bar charts, are easily interchangeable, but other chart types, like line and pie charts, are not.

Chart Styles

To quickly format a chart, you can choose from the Chart Styles section of the Chart Tools Design tab. This section has various layout options for each chart type that include different fills, backgrounds, labels, etc.

You can hold your mouse over each one to see it applied to your chart. Click on an option to keep it.

I personally tend not to like most of the choices, but it can be a good way to get close to what you want and then you can edit to a final layout from there.

Quick Layout

There is also a Quick Layout dropdown menu in the Chart Layouts section of the Chart Tools Design tab. These quick layouts generally involve different label arrangements and data displays. If you hold your mouse over each one you'll see it applied to your chart and also see a description of what attributes are included in that layout.

You can apply both a Chart Style and a Quick Layout to a chart, but the order in which you do so may impact the appearance and which attributes are kept and which are overwritten. I just took two identical charts and applied the same Chart

Style and Quick Layout to both of them but in different orders. The results were similar but one ended up with narrower columns, the legends on the two charts were in different locations, and one of the two had major gridlines while the other didn't. All because of the order in which I applied the two choices.

Change Colors

If you just want to mix up the colors in your chart, there are a number of pre-formatted options available under the Change Colors option in the Chart Styles section of the Chart Tools Design tab.

If you're working with one of the PowerPoint templates, the list of choices will use your theme colors. You can choose Colorful (multiple colors) or Monochromatic (different shades of one color) options.

Chart Elements

Charts come with a variety of optional elements that you can add, edit, or remove. This includes axes, axis titles, chart titles, data labels, data tables, error bars, gridlines, legends, series lines, trendlines, or up/down bars. Which ones are available depends on the chart type.

To edit your chart elements, go to the Add Chart Element dropdown menu in the Chart Layouts section of the Chart Tools Design tab. (On the far left.)

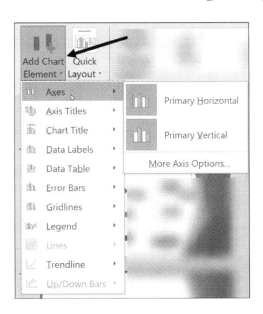

Elements that aren't available will be grayed out like Lines and Up/Down Bars are in the image above.

For each element where you can make a change there will be a secondary dropdown menu like the one you can see above for Axes.

The More Options choice will open a formatting task pane for that element that gives even more choices, but the dropdowns usually work for adding or removing an element.

To give you a few examples of what you can do here:

I will often add a Data Table with Legend Keys to my charts so that I can see a table of the actual data below the chart. When I do this, I also make sure to set the Legend to None because the information is already in the data table since it includes legend keys.

Also, for pie charts I usually want to include the Data Labels and I usually do so at the Outside End so that I can see what value is represented by each slice in the pie. I also often change the data labels so they display percentages instead of values. I do so using the task pane label options:

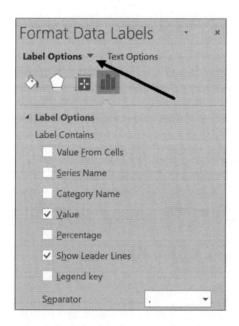

The Formatting Task Panes

To open the formatting task panes, you have a number of choices. You can click on More Options for any of the secondary element dropdown menus. Or you can right-click on your chart and choose the Format X option from the dropdown menu where X will be something like Data Labels, Data Series, Chart Area, Chart Title, etc. It all depends on where you're clicked on at the time.

No matter how you get there, once you have the task pane open you can move around to other formatting options for that chart or slide.

To do so, change the dropdown under the name of the task pane to what you need and then poke around to find where the particular formatting option you want is located.

So above where I wanted percentages to show instead of actual values, I had to choose "Series Sales Data Labels" from the dropdown menu and then click over to the Label Options image at the end of the four available icons.

Once there I could then check and uncheck what data to display for each pie slice.

If the task pane is already open you should be able to click onto your chart where you want to make your edit and the task pane should update to show formatting options for that part of the chart. But sometimes there's more than one option it could display, so that will get you close to what you need, but may not always get you exactly what you need.

As I mentioned, I use the task pane to change my pie chart labels to percentages. I also use it to "explode" a pie chart so that the individual slices have distance between them. And to rotate a pie chart so that the slices in the chart are where they look best visually.

Custom Colors

The color formatting we've covered so far is all quick hits. Pick a style, change colors from a pre-defined list of choices, etc.

But you can also change the colors or effects for any item in your chart to anything you want. You do this using the Shape Fill, Shape Outline, and Shape Effects choices available in the Chart Tools Format tab.

Both Shape Fill and Shape Outline will have dropdown menus that show sixty theme colors chosen to work with your theme and the ten standard colors, but you can always choose the More Colors option to use a different color.

For pie chart slices, bar charts, and column charts you should click on a segment and then choose a color from the Shape Fill dropdown.

In column and bar charts all segments for that particular data should be selected when you click on one of them. So here, for example, both of the Series 1 columns were automatically selected when I clicked on the left-hand column. You can see the circles at each corner that show they're currently selected.

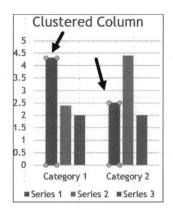

Once you're sure that the segment you want to change has been selected (and nothing else has), then you can pick your color from the Shape Fill dropdown.

For Line and Scatter charts, you have to use the Shape Outline dropdown menu instead.

You can also change your fill colors using the formatting task pane.

Filter Your Results

Click on your chart and you will see what looks like a little funnel off to the side. This is the Chart Filters option and will let you choose which data points appear in your chart if you don't want all of your data to display.

Format Chart Title and Other Text

To format text within a chart you can just select it like normal text and then use the text formatting options in the Font section of the Home tab. Just click into that text box and then make your formatting choices.

Resize A Chart

To resize a chart, you can click on the white boxes in the corners or on the sides and drag to the desired size.

You can also specify an exact size in the Size section of the Chart Tools Format tab.

Or you can go to the Format Chart Area task pane and in the Size & Properties section under Chart Options click on the Size arrow and then specify your values there.

The Format Chart Area pane also includes an option for specifying the exact position of your chart on your slide under the Position option in that same section.

Your other option is to click and drag the chart into position instead, but if you have multiple slides with charts on them this could create some disjointedness between slides as the charts appear to jump around from slide to slide.

If you have multiple charts on the same slide you can align them by dragging them into position. Dotted red lines will appear when the charts are aligned with one another.

Resize Chart Elements

When you resize a chart, all of the elements within the chart will also resize. So the title, the legend, the chart itself, will all adjust so that everything still fits nicely. But you can also resize just one chart element by clicking on it until you see it surrounded by a box with circles in the corners and then clicking and dragging on one of those circles.

Move Chart Elements

You can also move chart elements around. Once you've selected a specific chart element, like the chart title, you can left-click and drag to relocate it. Just be sure you're clicked onto a chart element and not the entire chart or you'll move the entire chart instead. Also, not all elements can be moved on their own. Titles and legends, yes. Axis labels, no.

* * *

Okay. Hopefully that gave you a solid overview on working with charts in PowerPoint. As I mentioned before, it's all based on how you'd work with charts in Excel, so if there's ever anything you can't figure out how to do when searching for help in PowerPoint also check Excel's help. And if you're familiar with charts in Excel you should be fine working in PowerPoint and vice versa.

Now on to SmartArt, which is like charts on steroids.

SmartArt

At its best SmartArt allows you to elevate a presentation to another level through the use of slick visual imagery. At its worst SmartArt creates confusion and looks pretentious.

So use it with care and consideration.

One of the biggest mistakes I see with using SmartArt is failing to understand that the graphic in question has a directionality to it or a flow to the numbers.

For example, there is a basic pyramid that you can insert using SmartArt. PowerPoint says you should use this pyramid "to show proportional, interconnected, or hierarchical relationships with the largest component on the bottom and narrowing up."

But I have seen this image used to show non-related values on the same slide. I've also seen it used where the largest value was on the top in the smallest segment.

And I've also seen where the first two levels of the pyramid were one related set of numbers and the third level was a completely different number.

Do not do that.

Only use SmartArt when the visual representation helps others to understand the point you're trying to make. If it doesn't do that, find a different way to present your information.

Okay. Now that the lecture is over, let's cover how you actually insert SmartArt into a presentation.

Insert SmartArt

One option is to click onto your slide and then go to the Illustrations section of the Insert tab and click on SmartArt.

This will bring up the Choose a SmartArt Graphic dialogue box:

Another option is to use a content-type slide and click on the Insert a SmartArt Graphic image in the top row of choices. (It's the one with a bright-green two-dimensional arrow behind a text box.)

A third option, if you already have your text listed on your slide, is to select your text and then go to the Paragraph section of the Home tab, click on the Convert to SmartArt dropdown arrow, and then choose the SmartArt option you want from there.

(I'd usually recommend against that last option because chances are you didn't list your information in the order or format that will work with the SmartArt graphic you want to use and you're probably just better off creating the graphic from scratch. But it's there as an option if you want to try it.)

Choose and Insert Your SmartArt Graphic

Okay. So let's say you used the Insert tab and chose SmartArt under the Illustrations section and now you have the Choose a SmartArt Graphic dialogue box showing.

On the left-hand side of the dialogue box are the categories of SmartArt. There are graphics for lists, processes, cycles, hierarchies, relationships, matrices, and pyramids. There is also a section for pictures where you can incorporate a picture into a SmartArt graphic with additional analysis or comment boxes around that picture. The final category, Office.com, includes a few additional options.

As you click on each category there will be a number of possible options displayed in the center of the dialogue box.

Click on one of those options and you will see on the right-hand side of the dialogue box a sample of the graphic and a description of what it should be used for, like here for a basic pyramid:

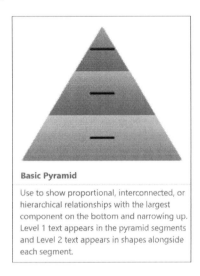

To select that option, click on OK in the bottom right corner of the dialogue box.

PowerPoint will then insert a template of that SmartArt graphic into your presentation. If you're using a theme, the colors used for the SmartArt graphic should match the theme you're using.

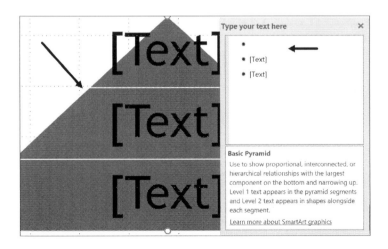

Add Your Text

At the same time that PowerPoint inserts your SmartArt graphic it should also open a Type Your Text Here dialogue box that shows sample text. (Like above where there are three bulleted points.)

Click into that dialogue box and replace the Text entries with your own values. This will overwrite the [Text] fields in the graphic like here where I replaced the three bullet points that said Text with Buyers, Prospects, and Potential Audience.

If that dialogue box isn't visible, you can just click onto the [Text] entries in the image itself and edit them there as well.

If you have a lot of text, though, it's easier to edit it in the dialogue box. To open that dialogue box when it isn't currently available, click on Text Pane in the Create Graphic section of the SmartArt Tools Design tab. This is especially true of situations where you want to add or delete additional entries.

To add an additional entry, just hit Enter on the last line of text. You should see another bullet point appear and you can just type in your text and a new element will be added to your graphic with that text.

Format Text and Elements

As you add or remove entries, the text should resize for you, but sometimes it doesn't resize enough for me like above with Buyers which is too big to fit on the interior of that section of the pyramid. Also, I sometimes find that I want to change the default font color or the fill color.

For example, above I don't like the black text on a dark background and I also don't like having each layer the exact same color. I think it would look better if each layer were a separate color.

To edit the text you can use the Font section of the Home tab just like you would for any other text entry. Use Ctrl + A to select all of the text at once if you want to change all of your text or select all of the text in an individual entry to change just that one entry.

To change the fill color of the elements in your graphic, the easiest way is to go to the SmartArt Tools Design tab and use the Change Colors dropdown menu. It has a number of pre-styled choices that use your theme colors.

For me that didn't work here because I wanted the bottom of the pyramid to be the darkest color and they didn't have an option for that. So instead I went to the SmartArt Tools Format tab and choose a different Shape Fill color for each of my elements.

As long as you choose your colors from the same Theme Colors column they will be complementary to one another.

The Format Shape text pane also allows you to change your Shape Fill. You can open it by right-clicking on the graphic and choosing Format Shape.

After I made my changes, here's what I ended up with:

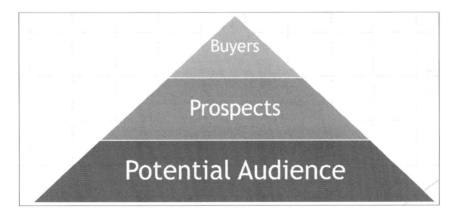

Not perfect. I don't like where the placement of Buyers is in that top section and I had to go with a slightly darker fill there to keep using white text throughout, but I think it looks much better than the default that had black text and just one color for all of the segments.

Change SmartArt Graphic

That's much better, but I think if I were using this for an actual presentation I'd want to use a different graphic. One option is a reverse pyramid, like this:

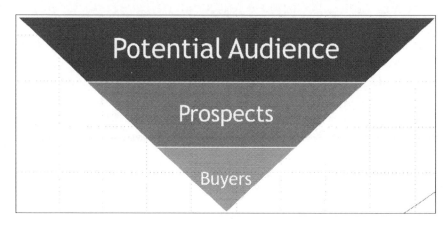

But I actually think that a process flow graphic is the better choice here. Something like this:

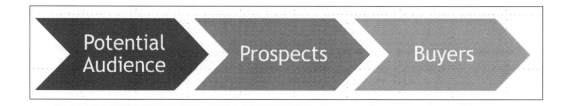

I lose the size component, but it does a better job of showing how you move from a potential audience to prospects to buyers.

To change your SmartArt graphic, click on the existing graphic and then go to the SmartArt Tools Design tab and choose a new option from the Layouts section. You can expand the entire section and click on More Layouts at the bottom if you need to move from one category of graphic to another like I did above.

I'd recommend that you do this immediately and not when you've done a lot of additional formatting because when you change your graphic it will reset to the original fonts, element fill colors, etc. So the images you see above are after I redid the changed font color, font size, and fill color. It didn't carry over. Also, I had to move around my text for both compared to the original.

SmartArt Effects

Another option you have is SmartArt Effects. For example, you can give a three-dimensional appearance or even directionality to some of the images.

The easiest way to do this is using the SmartArt Styles in the SmartArt Tools Design tab. Be careful, because that will overwrite any fill colors you've applied so if you're going to use one apply it first and then adjust your fill colors.

You can also use the Shape Effects dropdown in the Smart Art Tools Format tab. Be sure with this one to select all of your segments before you apply your effect or it will just apply to one element at at time.

Here I applied a SmartArt Style called Brick Scene to my process flow and then used Change Colors to apply different colors to each chevron:

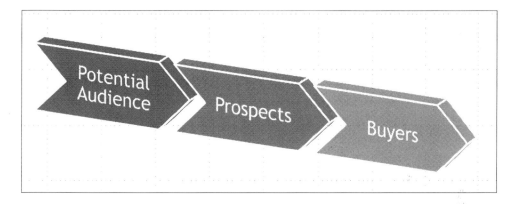

Notice that this is now three-dimensional and has more directionality to it than the original graphic did.

A Few More Options

There are a few more options for what you can do with SmartArt graphics to edit them. Let me walk through those real quick.

Convert To Text

In the Reset section of the Design tab you have an option to Convert To Text which will take your SmartArt graphic and turn it into text entries. This can be useful when you have a lot of text edits to make, but it does mean you will have to start over with the formatting of your graphic if you change it back to SmartArt.

Reset SmartArt

To reset the graphic back to the default settings that were in place when you inserted it you can use Reset Graphic from the Reset section of the SmartArt Tools Design tab. This will remove any color changes or effects you've added.

Move Up/Move Down

If you want to change the order of the components in your graphic, you can use the Move Up and Move Down options in the Create Graphic section of the SmartArt Tools Design tab.

That will move whichever segment you're clicked onto one segment forward or backward in the hierarchy. (If it's a pyramid it will actually move it up or down. If it's a process flow like we looked at above it will move it left or right.)

Change Direction

Clicking on Right To Left in the Create Graphic section of the SmartArt Tools Design tab will change the direction of any arrows in your graphic.

Demote/Promote

If you want to keep the information from one of your steps in your slide, but have it turned into a bullet point instead, you can click on it and then use the Demote option in the Create Graphic section of the SmartArt Tools Design tab.

To turn bulleted text into an element in your graphic, select the text and then click on Promote in that same section.

This is also a short-cut way to add additional items to your graphic. So, for example, I was able to demote one of my steps to a bullet point, then hit enter to get another bullet point, type in the text for that new bullet point, and then Promote both of the bullet points back into the graphic.

Add or Change Shapes

You are not stuck with the default shapes that are used in the SmartArt Graphic you choose. To change the shape for all of your elements at once, use Ctrl + A to select all of them and then go to the Shapes section of the SmartArt Tools Format tab under Change Shape and choose a different shape.

You can do the same for each individual element as well.

To move around the shapes in your graphic, select them and then click and drag them to where you want them.

You can also use shapes to add more elements to your graphic. Simply click on Add Shape in the top left corner of the Create Graphic section of the Design tab. That will add another element immediately after the element you currently have selected. Then you just have to right-click on the new element, choose Edit Text, and type in your new text.

Here is an example where I've changed the shape of my chevron process flow elements, added two new levels to the graphic, and also moved the elements around to create more of a downward flow from one step to the next:

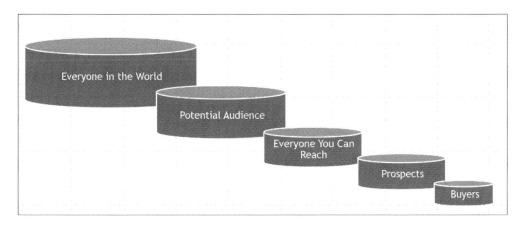

You can also copy any element and paste it back into the graphic to add another level.

Basically, if you have a vision for what you want to create, you can probably do it with SmartArt. Just remember that absolute power corrupts absolutely…

Avoid Confusion

At this point I feel obligated to remind you yet again that graphics in a presentation should be there to assist you in delivering your message but you need to be careful that they don't distract from that message.

Someone should be able to look at a SmartArt graphic in your presentation and just with a glance understand what you're trying to convey.

They shouldn't have to sit there and puzzle out why that graphic was used with that information.

For example, in the image below I've changed the last item to Cost of Production from Buyers. So now it flows from Potential Audience to Prospects to Cost of Production:

If I saw this image on a screen, you could be saying whatever you wanted, I'd be off on a mental tangent trying to figure out how you have a process flow that goes from Potential Audience to Prospects to Cost of Production.

Isn't Cost of Production part of a different flow? Doesn't that need to be with other finance-related fields? Why is it with potential audience?

Same issue if those arrows there on the chevrons were reversed. How do buyers flow to prospects? Huh.

Or if with the pyramids we had the buyers as the biggest layer. Shouldn't the potential audience be bigger than those who actually buy?

Use a bad graphic, you will lose your audience.

(I know, I'm just a stick in the mud. But remember, most of your bosses and clients probably are, too.)

* * *

Anyway. Enough of my forcing my opinions on you. But just think of all the time and energy that could be saved if we were all spared bad presentations.

Ah, that world would be amazing, wouldn't it?

Okay, then. Now on to Videos.

Videos

Insert Video is one of the options you have in your content slide defaults. It's in the bottom row and is an image of a strip of film. Click on that to bring up the Insert Video dialogue box which will let you navigate to the location on your computer where your video file is stored.

You can also insert a video using the Video dropdown in the Media section of the Insert tab. That allows you to choose between inserting a video that is stored on your device or one that is available online.

Choosing to insert a video from your device will open a navigation dialogue box. Choosing an online video will open a dialogue box where you can paste in the website address for that video. According to the Help documentation, PowerPoint 2019 supports videos from YouTube and Vimeo and requires use of Internet Explorer 11.

Also, since online videos play directly from those websites, they will only work if you have internet access and will be governed by the playback controls of those sites.

Finally, as the reminder in the bottom left corner of the dialogue box for inserting an online video says, "your use of online videos is subject to each provider's Terms of Use and Privacy Policy." Remember, there is such a thing as copyright and using someone else's material without valid permissions can be a costly mistake.

I'd generally advise that you try to use your own videos as much as possible to avoid any potential issues of that nature.

Okay, then. Whichever option you choose, find the video you want and insert it into your presentation by clicking on OK. Once you do so you should then see a still image from the video.

Hold your mouse over the video and you should see play buttons below it.

Play Video

Click on the play button on the left-hand side to play the video. When your video is playing that button will then turn to a pause button which you can click on if you need to pause the video.

There are also volume controls, a time counter, and the ability to move forward or backward in small increments (.25 seconds at a time).

When you navigate away from the slide with the video on it and come back to it, you may not see the play button below the video. If that happens simply move your mouse over the image to make it reappear.

During a presentation the play bar will appear as part of the bottom edge of the image instead of below it.

Change Video Screenshot

You can resize the video by clicking on it and then left-clicking and dragging on the white boxes along the perimeter. Use the white boxes in the corners to resize the image proportionately. Or you can use the Size section of the Video Tools Format tab. This will change the image proportionately.

Another option is to right-click on the video and choose Format Video from the dropdown to bring up the Format Video task pane. The Size section under Size & Properties will allow you to change the image size.

Video Tools Format Tab

Most video formatting options are limited to your own videos and will not work with the online videos, at least during replay.

The Video Styles section of the Video Tools Format tab lets you place borders or other effects around the video.

You can also apply a shape to your video using the Video Shape dropdown in that same section. If you do so, your video will play within a circle or arrow, etc.

The Adjust section has options where you can fix the brightness/contrast in the video, recolor it, or add a poster frame around the edges. Each dropdown menu shows a thumbnail of the available options.

Video Tools Playback Tab

In the Video Options section of the Video Tools Playback tab you have the choice of having the video play in automatically when the slide is presented, only when clicked upon, or in a designated order based upon when the other items in the slide appear.

You can also set the video to play full screen, loop until it's stopped, hide while not playing, or rewind after playing.

You can also control the volume, so for example if you wanted to mute the video, you could. Your sound options are low, medium, high, and mute. This would be separate from the computer's overall volume settings.

The Caption Options section allows you to link to a caption file for the video to allow for accessibility.

And the Editing section has options for trimming the video so that only a portion plays or adding a fade in or fade out.

Delete A Video

To delete the video, just click on it and then use the Delete key.

* * *

Alright. That's the basics of videos. One final caution about using your own videos in a presentation. If you insert your own video this will embed the video into your presentation which will substantially increase the file size.

Also, if you then distribute the presentation to others you could lose control over the video. (You will still own the copyright, but people are not always good about honoring that.)

But the biggest issue with using videos is having a quality video to begin with. No matter how much I wish it could, PowerPoint can't fix poorly shot, unedited videos of your dog.

Okay then. On to online pictures, 3D models, and icons.

Online Pictures, 3D Models, and Icons

The other three options that you have on a basic content slide are to insert online pictures, icons, and 3D Models.

Online Pictures

When using online pictures this means you're using someone else's image so I will remind you that copyright issues and trademark issues can be incredibly costly if you misstep. When you click on this option and then click on a category of images, you will see that there is a Creative Commons Only checkbox that is checked at the top.

I would recommend that you do not uncheck that box. Because if those photos are legitimately available under a creative commons license, then you are in fact free to use them. (Keep in mind that sometimes people steal an image and then upload it and indicate it is free to use, but they weren't the original creator so they can't do that, so as with all things online, proceed with caution. The bigger the audience for your presentation, the more you risk.)

You can also access the Online Pictures option using the Images section of the Insert tab. Choose Online Pictures from there.

Clicking on either option will bring up a web-based dialogue box that allows you to either search Bing or to find an image in your OneDrive account.

The dialogue box contains a series of categories you can click on or you can use the search bar to perform a keyword-based search for what you want.

Once you've performed a basic search or clicked onto a category there will be a small funnel located above the images and just below the search box. Click on that to specify the image size, type, layout, and color you want.

If you see an image you want to use, click on it, and then choose Insert from the bottom corner of the dialogue box and it will be inserted into your presentation.

Once the image is in your presentation you can use the Picture Tools Format tab to edit the image as needed.

3D Models

PowerPoint 2019 also allows you to insert 3D Models into your presentation. These models take an image in 3D and let you rotate the image to see all angles.

3D Models can be great for something like a chemistry class where you need to visualize what a certain molecule actually looks like. And I know something like this would've helped a few friends during geometry class. But I'd also warn that something like this can be seen as gimmicky if used for the wrong audience.

To insert one, either click on the 3D Models option in a content slide or go to the Illustrations section of the Insert tab and click on the dropdown arrow under 3D Models.

If you have your own model you'll need to use the dropdown and choose This Device.

If you don't have your own model choose Stock 3D Models from the dropdown or use the content slide option. This will open a web-linked dialogue box that shows a variety of categories you can choose from such as emojis, chemistry, anatomy, clothing, furniture, industrial, etc. You can also do a keyword search using the search box up top.

(It appears that these 3D models are generated by Microsoft so it is likely you won't have any copyright issue using them in a presentation. (And they seem to actively encourage users to modify and create their own 3D images.) However, if I were going to present to a very large audience or worked for a large company, I would still double-check that I had permissions to use these models first.)

Once you've found a model you want to use, click on it and then click on Insert at the bottom of the dialogue box which will place the model into your presentation.

Once you've inserted a 3D model into your slide, it will have a circular image on top with looping lines in two circles, one up and down and one side to side. Click on that image, hold the click, and move your cursor to rotate the image.

When you click on the model there will also be a 3D Model Tools Format tab that you can access that lets you reset the model to its original position, choose a specific model view, change the positioning of the model on the page, or change its size.

Icons

Icons are your final option for what you can insert from a content slide. They are basically little images that are like fancy line drawings of various subjects.

If you've ever seen the little man and woman images on a bathroom sign somewhere you know what an icon is.

You can insert an icon into your presentation by either clicking on the bird with a leaf image in the bottom right of the second row of choices on a slide or by using the Icons option in the Illustrations section of the Insert tab.

Clicking on either choice will open a web-linked Insert Icons dialogue box where you can search or choose icons from a variety of categories such as accessibility, analytics, animals, apparel, arrows, arts, etc.

Once more it appears these are ones designed by Microsoft so they should be fine for use in a presentation. But if you use them commercially in some way you may get into trouble, so once more consider consulting with a lawyer if you have big money to lose or high visibility.

(A presentation for your high school class of ten should be fine. One for a Fortune 100 company's annual report? Eh…Double-check. Both would be equally problematic if there is a problem, but one is much more likely to be noticed than the other.)

To insert an icon into your presentation, click on it, and then click on Insert.

Icons are smaller than the other items you can insert into a presentation, but you can resize them just like anything else.

Once inserted, you can click on your icon to see the Graphic Tools Format tab which will let you change the fill, outline, or effects of the icon just like you would with any shape.

Use Graphics Fill to change the color of your icon. Your default choices in the dropdown should match the theme you're using.

Master Slides: Just a Quick Note

Alright…

So we just covered a number of items you can insert into a presentation.

Now we need to talk about master slides. I mentioned them before in the context of editing the placement of your footer fields in your presentation. If you have a theme you like but the footers aren't where you want them, this is the best place to make that change.

But messing with your master slides can be dangerous because it impacts that entire template, so it's not something to do lightly. (And if it's a corporate template probably not something you should do at all.)

I would also recommend that if you're going to make changes to the master slides that you do so before you start to build your presentation. Otherwise you may have text that isn't fully visible or situations where some images or backgrounds update to show the changes you made and others don't.

Now that the warnings are out of the way, to see your master slides go to the Master Views section of the View tab, and click on the Slide Master option.

This will take you to the master slide for the type of content slide you were on at the time you made that selection.

If you look in the left-hand navigation pane you'll also see thumbnails for all master slides that are part of the theme. Remember all those layouts we walked through in *PowerPoint 2019 Beginner?* That's what those thumbnails are, one per layout.

To apply a change to just that slide layout, you can edit the slide you're on. But chances are you'll want to apply that change to all of the slide layouts. To do that, click on the very top thumbnail image in the left-hand pane instead. It should be offset to the left of the other slides in the task pane.

Any change you make to this master master slide will carry through to all the other slides that are listed below it.

For example, if you rearrange the position of your footer elements in this slide you should see that those footer elements also change in all of the other slides layouts.

When you click on that slide it will appear in your main workspace and you can click and drag the elements around just like you would with any slide. It's just that any changes you make here apply to every slide in your presentation.

Use the Background section of the Slide Master tab to change the overall appearance of your presentation. For example, you can use the Color dropdown menu there to change the color palette for your template to one of the twenty-plus color palettes that are shown or even to create a new color palette for the presentation.

(As you hold your mouse over each one the presentation should change in the background to let you see what it will look like.)

If you do change your master slides, I'd recommend that you Rename it using the Edit Master section so that you don't overwrite something you didn't intend to.

But, honestly, we're on the edge of advanced PowerPoint here so I'm not going to go into this in more detail, I just wanted you to know that the option existed in case you ever need it..

Select All

You can select all of your slides or all of the objects on a slide using the Select All option.

The easiest way to use Select All is through the control shortcut, Ctrl + A.

To select all of the text in a text box, click into the text box first.

To select all of the objects on a slide, click somewhere outside a text box first.

To select all of your slides, click on a slide thumbnail image in the left-hand navigation pane first.

For text the text will be highlighted in gray. For objects you'll see boxes around each shape/image. For slides you'll see a red border around each slide thumbnail image in the navigation pane.

Another option for selecting all is to go to the Editing section of the Home tab and then choose Select All or Select Objects from the dropdown menu.

Sections

It is possible to split a presentation into multiple sections. PowerPoint recommends doing this to allocate tasks between team members, for example. It also makes it easier to move slides around because you can collapse a section and then click and drag that whole section to a new location in the presentation.

If you have a very lengthy presentation it can also make navigating the presentation a lot easier if you use sections and collapse them. Like so:

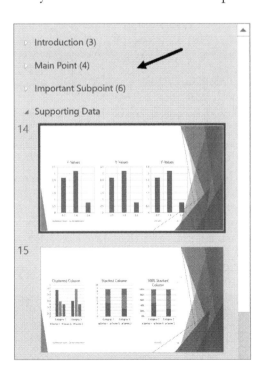

M.L. Humphrey

You can see that I have three sections that are collapsed (Introduction, Main Point, and Important Subpoint) before the current section called Supporting Data. There are thirteen slides in those other sections that I've hidden by collapsing the sections. (The number of slides in each section is in parens at the end of the section name.)

If I needed to see the three introductory slides I could do so by expanding that section. If all slides were visible I'd have to scroll up to see them and wouldn't also be able to see the thumbnails of the slides in my current section.

To insert a section, right-click onto the space in the left-hand navigation pane directly above the slide thumbnail where you want to start your new section and choose Add Section from the dropdown menu.

This will insert a new section starting with that slide. You should also see a dialogue box called Rename Section that shows a section name of Untitled Section. Type over that name to give the section the name you want to use.

If you don't change the section name immediately, you can always right-click on the name and choose Rename Section from the dropdown menu later to bring up that dialogue box.

Either way, click on Rename once you've entered your text.

There are other options available for sections once you've created one as you can see here, just right-click on the section name:

Remove Section will remove the section name but keep the slides. Remove Section & Slides will remove both. Remove All Sections will remove all section names but keep the slides.

Move Section Up or Move Section Down will move the entire section, including its slides. Collapse All will hide all slides but show the section names. Expand All will show all slides as well as section names.

These options are also available in the Slide section of the Home tab under the Section dropdown menu.

88

Comments

It is always a good idea when working on a draft document with others to keep any comments or questions out of the body of the document. In PowerPoint you can do this using Comments.

To insert a comment, go to the point in the presentation where you want to make the comment and either right-click and choose New Comment from the dropdown menu, or click onto that location and then go to the Comments section of the Review tab and choose New Comment.

This will open the Comments pane on the right-hand side of the workspace. Your user name will appear above a white text box. Type your comment there.

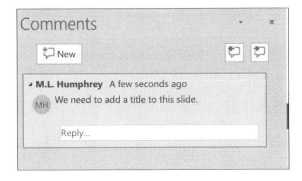

Once entered, each comment will show who made it and when.

On the presentation slide a comment is represented by a small quote bubble in a peach-sort of color.

Click to add title

Click on that comment bubble to open the Comments task pane and see the text of the comment. If comments aren't visible you can also go to the Show Comments dropdown in the Comments section of the Review tab and check the box next to Comments Pane.

Comments will not show when you have the presentation in slide show mode, but I'd recommend that if you do use comments that you delete them before the final version is saved.

To do this, go to the Comments section of the Review tab, click on the Delete dropdown, and choose Delete All Comments in This Presentation.

To navigate between comments in a presentation you can either use the Previous and Next options in the Comments section of the Review tab, or their icons which are located at the top of the Comments pane. Previous looks like a comment bubble with a left-hand arrow in the top corner. Next looks like a comment bubble with a right-hand arrow in the top corner.

To reply to an existing comment type into the white text box directly below the comment which says "Reply…" in gray letters.

You can also make a new comment instead, but that's the old way and a messier option that sometimes doesn't maintain the thread of the conversation.

To edit an existing comment, click on the text of the comment and it will become a white text box again where you can then add to, delete, or edit the text.

Incorporate Group Edits

Unlike Word, PowerPoint does not have a track changes option. What they recommend doing instead is to save the original draft of your presentation and then save a renamed version of the presentation and make that renamed version available for people to add their comments or make their edits through a share site.

Once those edits or comments have been made to the second version of the presentation you can then bring them into the original version of the presentation and review them by using the Compare function.

I will note here that I personally think Compare is poorly-designed and do not use it myself, but I'm presenting it here so you know about it and how to use it.

So, having said that, to compare two presentations open the original version of the presentation in PowerPoint, go to the Compare section of the Review tab, and click on Compare.

This will open the Choose File to Merge with Current Presentation dialogue box. Navigate to where you have the second version of the presentation saved, select it, and then click on the Merge button.

You will now see your initial presentation with a Revisions pane on the right-hand side. For me it was a little small so I had to resize it by clicking along the edge and dragging to the left once I saw the two-sided arrow.

If there are no edits to the current slide it will tell you so and then tell you the next slide which does have edits. Like this:

If there are comments in the merged presentation you will see the Comments pane on the right-hand side as well. If there are no comments in the current slide it will say so but there will be previous and next navigation options to move to the next comment in the presentation.

For changes that were made to the presentation itself you can either navigate to the specified slide using the thumbnails in the navigation pane on the left-hand side of the screen or go to the Compare section of the Review tab and use the Next option.

(The Previous option will take you to any prior edits if you're in the middle of the presentation.)

This is also where you can open or close the Reviewing Pane.

Now, here's where it gets weird. It's all backwards how this works in my opinion. Because if someone has made edits to a presentation I want to see how it looks with those edits incorporated. But the default for Compare is to show the original presentation as it was before any edits were made.

The view of the current slide as you see it on the screen is how it existed in your original version. To see how it looks with the identified edits, click on the small image showing a piece of paper with a pencil in the top right corner of the slide. That will then show a description of the edit(s). Click on the box next to each edit description to then show the edit on the slide.

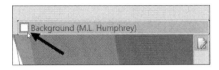

To remove the edit from your view, uncheck that box.

This is the strangest part: You can only accept an edit when the change is *not* visible on the slide.

You do this by either going to the Compare section of the Review tab, clicking on the Accept dropdown option, and then choosing Accept Change or by right-clicking on the little pencil with paper and choosing Accept Change from there.

Once you accept that change (that you couldn't see as you were accepting it), the change will then appear on the slide.

(Who came up with that, I do not know.)

At least they did set it up so that when a change is visible, you can reject it, which you do by going to the Compare section of the Review tab or by right-clicking and choosing the Reject option.

For changes that involve moving a slide to a new location or deleting a slide or a section, those will be flagged in the left-hand navigation pane, separate from changes that were made to an individual slide's content or format.

Honestly, I find this a very awkward way to review changes in a presentation. If I were faced with a situation like this what I would likely do, assuming I trusted my team not to make crazy edits that I needed to know about, would be to immediately accept all of the changes in the presentation and then review the presentation as if it was supposed to be a final version. (Which is basically just reviewing the second version of the presentation without ever having to Compare the two versions.)

Compare is nice in the sense that it will keep you from missing any changes that were made that can slip by and will let you know who made that change, but it's really messy how they've set it up.

Zoom and Views

We've pretty much covered the big ticket items you need to know to work at an intermediate level in PowerPoint, but I wanted to cover a few little clean up items before we wrap up.

First, let's look at how to use Zoom and what the different Views options are.

Zoom

On occasion, you may want to increase the size of the slide you're viewing or you may want to decrease its size. This can be done using Zoom.

The easiest way to do this is to use the slider in the bottom right corner of PowerPoint. You'll see a negative sign, a line with a midpoint marked and a rectangle perpendicular to that line, and then a plus sign and a percentage value.

Click on the rectangle to drag to the desired zoom level or click on the line on either side of the rectangle to move in the desired direction. By default I tend to have my slides around 85-90% which makes each slide fully visible on my screen.

You can also click on the plus and minus marks at either end of the line to move up or down to the nearest 10% mark. So originally you'll move from 85% to 80% or 90% but then you'll move to 70% or 100% and so on.

If you resize the PowerPoint window to be less than the full screen this may require you to adjust your zoom level to still see your full slide.

Your other option is to go to the Zoom section of the View tab and click on Zoom. This will bring up the Zoom dialogue box. You can type a percentage value into the Percent box or use the up and down arrows there to change the value. Or you can click into one of the white circles to select a pre-listed value. Your choices are Fit, 400%, 200%, 100%, 66%, 50%, and 33%.

Choosing a value that is greater than your current value will make the slide on your screen larger. Choosing a value that is less than your current value will make it smaller. The panes on either side will not change size, just the main workspace.

Click OK to actually apply your zoom level.

If you zoom to the point where you can't see the entire slide then scroll bars will appear on the bottom and right side of the slide image so that you can scroll to see the entire slide.

You can return your slide to a size that will fit the available space by clicking on Fit to Window in the Zoom section of the View tab or by choosing Fit in the dialogue box.

Views

Normal View

You can also change your default slide view if you want. This is done by selecting one of the options in the Presentation Views section of the View tab.

The default, or Normal, view shows the one slide that you're currently on in the center of the screen with a navigation pane on the left-hand side that contains thumbnails of the other slides in your presentation. If you have notes on your presentation, those will appear at the bottom.

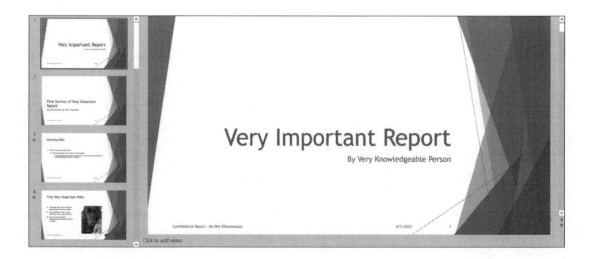

Outline View

Outline View, the next option, replaces the thumbnails in the presentation with the text from each slide shown in a bulleted or list format. You can click on that text and delete, edit, or add to it but not format it. In this view, the current presentation slide is still visible on the right half of the screen, but it's smaller and the notes section below the slide remains.

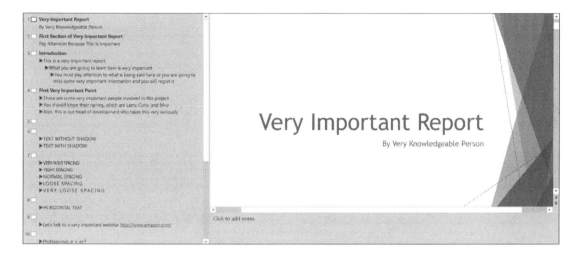

This view is good for quickly reviewing or editing the text in your presentation, but it's not going to show you images or layout in that section.

According to PowerPoint "[w]orking in Outline view is particularly handy if you want to make global edits, get an overview of your presentation, change the sequence of bullets or slides, or apply formatting changes."

Slide Sorter

The Slide Sorter view shows you thumbnails of all of your slides but no central slide to edit.

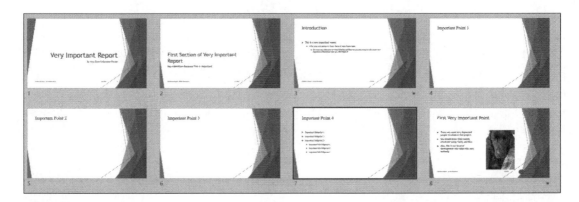

This is probably the most useful view for moving slides around within your presentation. The big advantage of this view over the Normal view is that you have more slides visible. Combine this view with Zoom Out and you can see approximately seventy slides at once.

To move a slide, left-click and drag it to where you want it. When you do this, all other slides will move over to accommodate the slide you moved.

You can also select multiple slides by clicking on one slide and then either holding down Ctrl and clicking on individual slides or Shift and clicking on the first or last slide in the series you want to select. Once your slides are selected, left-click and drag the entire set of selected slides to their new location.

Rather than click and drag the slides you can also use Copy (Ctrl +C) or Cut (Ctrl + X) and Paste (Ctrl + V) to move the slides around.

Notes Page

The next view, the Notes Page view, will show you the slide and any notes for that slide as they will appear when printed. You can actually click into the text box for the notes in this view and add or edit your notes.

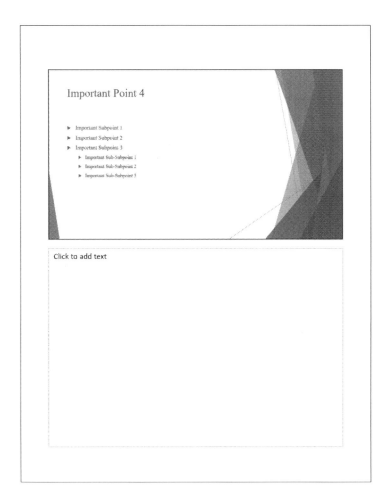

(If all you want is to know what notes you have on a slide, the easier option is to stay in the Normal view and just click on Notes in the status bar at the bottom of the screen. Click on Notes again to hide your notes from view.)

Reading View

The final view, the Reading View, shows you how the slide will look as part of a presentation, including any animations and transitions, without requiring that you view it as a full screen presentation.

In this view, you can use the arrows in the status bar at the bottom to move forward or backward through the presentation. You can also just click on the slide or use the arrow keys on your keyboard to move forward

Use Esc or left-click on Menu (which is between the two arrows in the status bar) and choose End Show to get back to the normal PowerPoint screen. You can also click on the Normal icon in the status bar next to the right arrow to get back to the Normal View.

Save As PDF

I covered how to save a file and how to change the format of that file when you save it in *PowerPoint 2019 Beginner*, but there are a few extra tips I wanted to share about saving a PowerPoint presentation as a PDF.

To save a PowerPoint presentation as a PDF file choose the Save As option.

Next, choose the location where you want to save the file. This will bring up the Save As dialogue box which includes a Save As Type dropdown menu at the bottom.

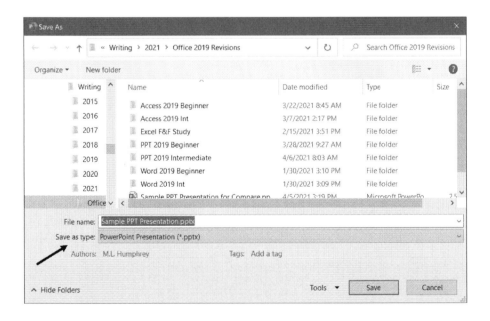

Click on the arrow for that dropdown menu and choose PDF, which is the fourth option down. Once you do this a box that says Options will appear below that dropdown menu. Click on it to see additional options related to PDF files.

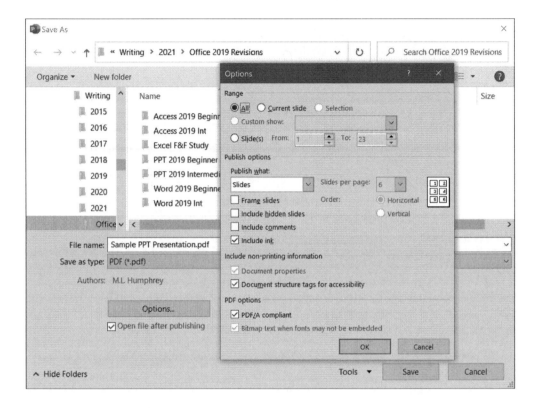

If you just want only the current slide to be saved as a PDF, click on Current Slide in the first row of options under Range.

If you want to save a set of slides but not the entire presentation as a PDF, use the Slide(s) option in the Range section and then type in the first slide number and last slide number for your range of slides.

If the slides you want to save are not continuous, then select them first using Ctrl and the navigation pane and then when you choose to Save As a PDF, use the Selection choice from the Range section. This will save your selected slides as a single PDF file.

Otherwise, just leave the Range option set to All.

You can also create a PDF of the handouts version of your presentation, the notes pages from the presentation, or the outline view of the presentation using the Publish What dropdown in the Publish Options section. Choosing handouts will let you specify the number of slides to include on each printed page.

The rest of the options can generally be left as-is unless you have a specific reason to change them.

Once you've made your selections click on OK and then click on Save to save your file as a PDF.

Another way to generate a PDF file of your presentation is by going to the File tab and using the Export option. From there you can choose to Create a PDF/XPS Document. It brings up a Publish as PDF or XPS dialogue box that looks the same as the Save As dialogue box except that the PDF file type is already selected and the Options button is over to the right.

Both approaches should give you a PDF file that meets your specifications.

Save As An Image

Another Save As option that I've used on occasion was the ability to save my presentation as images. This is because in the past I've used PowerPoint to create the images that I placed in my books. I would paste the screenshot I intended to use into a PowerPoint slide, add arrows and text, trim the image, and then export the result as a .jpg image I could insert into my presentation.

(As a side note, that's not the best way to do things, but it was the best way I knew how to do them at the time.)

Okay, so how do you do this?

To generate images of your PowerPoint slides, choose Save As, and then choose your location you want to save your file.

This will once more open the Save As dialogue box. This time you should choose GIF Graphics Interchange Format (*.gif), JPEG File Interchange Format (*.jpg), PNG Portable Network Graphics Format (*.png), or TIFF Tag Image File Format (*.tif) from the Save As Type dropdown menu.

Which image type you prefer is up to you. These days I tend to use the TIFF option, but there are places that will only accept a JPEG. For most uses it's really not going to make a difference, but if it does you have all the choices available.

Once you select an image file type and click on Save, PowerPoint is going to ask you, "Which slides do you want to export?"

If you choose All Slides it will create a new folder using the name you have the presentation saved under and will then save each individual slide as its own image file within that folder. It will name those files according to their slide number. So you'll have a folder named, for example, PowerPoint 2019 Intermediate with files inside it named Slide1, Slide2, etc.

If you choose Just This One instead, PowerPoint will save just the current slide as an image file using with the name of the presentation. So be careful there. You can think it saved it all as one file, but it didn't.

Slide Transitions

In *PowerPoint 2019 Beginner* I covered how to use animations to have only a portion of the text on a slide appear at a time. This can be very useful when doing a presentation so that the people you're talking to don't read ahead and stop listening to you.

I tend to have a strong dislike for most of the animations options where text spins onto the screen or wheels in or grows and turns, etc. It's usually not necessary and distracts from what you're trying to do.

Which is why I didn't cover the equivalent for slides, which are called Transitions. I'd generally recommend caution when using these.

I have seen them used effectively, however. I once attended a presentation on the psychology of evil that started with the presenter playing a timed presentation of images from a prisoner of war camp with some sort of sound effect each time the slide changed.

Five minutes of that drives the point home.

But in general? Approach with caution.

Okay, so how do you add transitions to slides?

Click on the slide in the left-hand pane that you want to transition to and then go to the Transitions tab and click on the transition type you want to use from the Transition To This Slide section.

As you click on your choice, PowerPoint will briefly show the transition in the main view portion of the screen. So you will see the prior slide transitioning to your current one using the selected transition type.

If you miss this demonstration or want to see it again, you can click on the Preview option on the left-hand side of the Transitions tab and it will run again.

If you want the transition to take more or less time, this can be adjusted in the

Timing section of the Transitions tab by changing the Duration.

If you want all of your slides to have the same transition settings that you've already applied to the current slide (duration, sound, type), click on Apply To All in the Timing section of the Transitions tab.

If you really want to annoy people, you can even add a sound to your slide transition. This is also under the Timing section of the Transitions tab. Choose the sound you want from the Sound dropdown. The sound will then play as the slide transitions. If you choose just a sound transition but no movement, you'll need to run the slide show or use the Reading View to hear it in action.

(And, again, I have seen sound transitions used effectively before, but not often. That *one* time is the only one I can remember.)

The Transitions tab is also where you can change the setting that advances a presentation to the next slide using a mouse click. That option is on by default.

You can instead set it to advance after a set period of time under the Advance Slide settings in the Timing section. This can be a good option for when you're using a series of images in a PowerPoint presentaiton as a background slide show on a computer screen while waiting to present, for example.

To see the timed transitions in action, you'll need to launch the slide show or use the Reading View.

And to apply the same timing to all of your slides, select them all first, and then specify the setting you want to use or check Apply to All when you're done.

Conclusion

Alright. That's it.

Hopefully you now have a better understanding of PowerPoint than you did when you started. However, as the name implies, this was not meant to be a comprehensive guide to PowerPoint. The basics of using PowerPoint were already covered in *PowerPoint 2019 Beginner* and there are some more advanced skills I didn't mention here at all or that I mentioned enough for you to know about but not in full and complete detail.

But at this point I hope you've learned enough about how PowerPoint works that you can find those additional answers on your own. PowerPoint, like all of Office, tends to follow a certain logic, so that when you don't know how to do something you can often figure it out based on how you did other similar tasks.

But there are also a number of excellent help options out there to assist you.

The first option is to go to the Help tab and click on Help, or use F1, to launch the PowerPoint Help task pane.

You will see some popular categories listed as well as a search box where you can type in what you're looking for. Using PowerPoint help will often lead you to the answer you need.

Within PowerPoint some of the menu choices also have a basic description which you can see if you just hold your mouse over them. In addition, some of those descriptions include a Tell Me More note at the bottom that you can click on to launch the specific help description for that option.

For example, if I go to the Text section of the Insert tab and hold my mouse over the WordArt dropdown it tells me that I can "add some artistic flair to my document using a WordArt text box" and then has Tell Me More at the bottom. If I click on that Tell Me More it takes me straight to the help section for Insert WordArt.

If the help options within PowerPoint are not enough, you can also do an internet search to find your answer. Be sure to include the version of PowerPoint you're working in and some keywords that are relevant to your search. I usually choose the support.office.com results first because I expect them to be the most official and reliable option. But if it's a "can you do this weird thing" question as opposed to a "how does this work" question, then sometimes you'll need to branch out to other sources.

Worst case scenario, there are a number of online user forums where you can ask a question.

Also, you're always welcome to reach out to me. Chances are I'll know the answer or be able to find it for you easily enough. Just send an email.

And that's that. Remember, the goal of a presentation is usually to convey information, so if whatever you're trying to do with your presentation doesn't accomplish that, then don't do it. PowerPoint is tremendously powerful and gives you all sorts of options, but that can be as dangerous as it is helpful. So keep it as clean and simple as you can. Don't let the appearance overwhelm the message.

Good luck with it.

INDEX

ABOUT THE AUTHOR

M.L. Humphrey is a former stockbroker with a degree in Economics from Stanford and an MBA from Wharton who has spent close to twenty years as a regulator and consultant in the financial services industry.

———————————————

You can reach M.L. at mlhumphreywriter@gmail.com or at mlhumphrey.com.

Made in the USA
Middletown, DE
21 November 2021